# THE CLASSIC BUSES
## Gavin Booth

FRASER STEWART BOOKS

The first of the really standardised buses, the LGOC B type. B214, which is now preserved, is seen at Hounslow in 1912, pioneering the new country route to peaceful riverside Staines.

CLASSIC BUSES

First published 1980

ISBN 1 874723 18 4

This edition published 1992 by Fraser Stewart Book
Wholesale Ltd, Abbey Chambers, 4 Highbridge Street,
Waltham Abbey, Essex EN9 1DQ, produced by
The Promotional Reprint Company Ltd, UK.

Printed in Czechoslovakia
50952

## Acknowledgements

My thanks are due firstly to the authors of many books and
magazine articles which have proved invaluable sources of
reference in preparing the material for this book. Articles in
*Buses Illustrated* (particularly those by Alan Townsin),
*Buses, Old Motor* and *The Omnibus Magazine* have proved
most useful, as have contemporary issues of the notable trade
papers *Commercial Motor* and *Motor Transport*.

Books which can be recommended for fuller details of the
models covered, and for further reading, are *The London
B-type Motor Omnibus* by G. J. Robbins and J. B. Atkinson;
*The Early Motor Bus* by Charles E. Lee; *Buses and
Trolleybuses before 1919* by David Kaye; *British
Double-Deckers since 1942* by Alan Townsin; *The Leyland
Bus* by Doug Jack; *Daimler Buses in Camera* by Stewart J.
Brown; *Feathers in Their Cap* by Robin Hannay; *Guy Buses
in Camera* by Jasper Pettie; *Bristol — a Century on the
Road* by Martin S. Curtis.

Many photographers supplied prints from which the
illustrations in this book were chosen. Where sources are
known, these are listed below.

*AEC:* 29, 33 (top), 34 (centre, foot), 35 (top, centre left, foot),
  36 (top, centre), 50 (top right), 83, 87 (foot), 88 (foot), 89
  (inserts).
*H. F. Adcock:* 33 (foot).
*Ian Allan Library:* Front endpapers, 10 (lower), 21, 27
  (lower), 31, 34 (top), 39 (upper), 40 (top, centre), 42 (top),
  43, 46, 47, 51, 52 (lower), 53 (lower), 54 (lower), 55
  (centre), 61, 63 (upper), 66, 67 (top), 75 (lower), 81
  (centre), 84 (lower), 85 (foot), 87 (centre), 88 (centre), 85
  (top right), 99 (2), 102, 112 (top), rear endpapers.
*G. H. F. Atkins:* 19 (top), 33 (centre), 35 (centre right), 42
  (foot), 45 (centre), 48 (lower), 49 (lower), 50 (top left), 58
  (lower), 77 (upper), 94 (top).
*Gavin Booth:* 20 (top right, centre), 59, 62 (lower), 72 (foot),
  88 (top), 90 (top), 105 (centre left).
*Gavin Booth Collection:* 19 (centre), 20 (top left), 25 (lower),
  32, 44 (2), 48 (upper), 56 (upper), 71 (top left), 79 (upper
  left), 95 (top left), 105 (foot), 113 (foot left).
*Stewart J. Brown:* 49 (upper), 50 (centre), 57 (upper), 82
  (top), 95 (foot), 96 (inset), 97 (foot), 104 (foot), 105 (centre
  right), 111 (top, centre).

*Stewart J. Brown Collection:* 39 (lower).
*G. Coxon:* 108 (upper).
*Crosville:* 19 (foot left).
*Michael Dryhurst:* 69 (top), 96 (main picture), 121 (centre
  left).
*Michael Fowler:* 81 (foot).
*Galleon Tours:* 89 (main picture).
*D. L. G. Hunter:* 56 (lower).
*Leyland:* 4, 19 (foot right), 23, 24 (top 2, centre), 25 (upper),
  26 (upper), 28 (foot), 73, 76 (2), 78, 79 (top right, centre,
  foot), 81 (top 2), 87 (top), 100 (lower), 101 (2), 106 (5),
  116 (2), 117, 118, 119 (lower), 120 (2), 121 (foot).
*London Transport:* 1/2, 5, 8, 9, 10 (upper), 11, 13, 14, 15 (2),
  16 (2), 84 (upper), 93 (lower).
*Lothian Region Transport:* 41 (upper), 90 (centre).
*Robert F. Mack:* 97 (4).
*G. R. Mills:* 45 (top), 68 (foot), 95 (centre), 98, 105 (top),
  109, 111 (foot).
*T. W. Moore:* 28 (top, centre), 37, 41 (lower left), 50 (foot),
  65, 69 (centre, foot), 71 (top right), 72 (top), 75 (upper), 77
  (lower), 82 (centre), 90 (foot), 91, 103, 104 (top), 107, 110,
  113 (centre), 114 (top), 121 (top).
*T. W. Moore Collection:* 41 (lower right), 52/53, 54 (upper).
*Don Morris:* 27 (upper), 42 (centre), 45 (foot), 55 (foot), 58
  (upper), 62 (upper), 63 (centre), 74, 93 (upper).
*A. Moyes:* 33 (top, inset), 64 (3), 94 (foot), 107 (foot right),
  112 (foot), 114 (centre), 115.
*A. J. Owen:* 24 (foot), 40 (foot).
*Jasper Pettie Collection:* 55 (top).
*Scottish Bus Group:* 36 (foot).
*Edward Shirras:* 85 (top).
*P. Sykes:* 94 (centre)
*M. J. Tozer:* 67 (3), 68 (top), 85 (centre).
*M. J. Tozer Collection:* 7 (2).
*Ulsterbus:* 100 (upper), 114 (foot).
*Viewfinder:* 63 (foot).
*George F. T. Waugh Collection:* 17.
*R. L. Wilson:* 20 (foot 2), 26 (lower), 57 (lower), 68 (centre),
  71 (centre foot), 72 (centre), 82 (foot), 97 (1), 104 (centre),
  108 (lower), 112 (centre), 113 (top), 119 (upper), 121
  (centre right).

# Contents

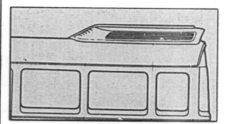

# Introduction

The word 'classic' can be defined in several different ways. Among others, *The Concise Oxford Dictionary* offers 'of the first class, of acknowledged excellence; remarkably typical, outstandingly important' — all of which could arguably refer to the buses in this book.

The 15 bus types described in these pages seem to merit the description 'classic'. They all either contributed in a material way to the development of the motor bus in Britain, or they entered service in significant numbers to become familiar in most parts of the country; some, indeed, are included on both counts. The London buses are exceptions to the rule — but over the years London buses have often been just that. Three London types, the B, RT and RM, are included in this book, and although initially their scope of activity was fairly restricted, their importance cannot be questioned. It could be argued that other London types could be included, but many have been developments of commercially-available chassis, unlike the B, RT and RM, and in all honesty do not merit inclusion.

Midland Red, the other big operator of 'home-made' vehicles, is not represented. Its designs have often been advanced, but were rarely produced in sufficiently large numbers to influence general design trends.

The vehicles which *are* included cover the motor bus from its dawning more than 75 years ago, right up to the epitome of 1970s standardisation, the Leyland National. Each one is fully described, and there is historical background on the manufacturers, together with details of contemporary, competing models.

The buses in this book tend to be remembered with affection — something which is not always the case. It is difficult to explain why several tons of wood, metal, glass and rubber can excite affection. For enthusiasts it may be pleasing design, distinctive sounds or memories of interesting journeys; for bus company engineers, recollections of economy and reliability. Whatever the reasons, certain bus types seem to attract almost universal affection — the Daimler COG5, London RT and Leyland PD2, for instance. The rugged Guy Arab attracted a different kind of respect, while the Leyland National so far only earns a grudging admiration from enthusiasts bemoaning the spread of standardisation.

There must be no doubt that this is my list. I fully realise that my readers will have their own nominations for the buses which can be called 'classic'. To ensure continuity, though, the chosen models follow design through the years, and I have attempted to avoid over-exposure of any single make. Sometimes this is difficult; AEC; Bristol and particularly Leyland have, in retrospect, made important contributions to the evolution of the bus, which is not to under-rate the significance of respected names like Albion, Crossley, Dennis, Ford, Gilford, Maudslay, Thornycroft or Tilling-Stevens. Given the available space, the selection included in these pages covers the most deserving models.

The classic buses, in fact.

Edinburgh                              **Gavin Booth**

*Below:* Classics of the 1950s — five lowbridge all-Leyland PD2/10s ready for delivery to Luton Corporation in 1953.

*Right:* The characteristic nose of the Milnes–Daimler 28hp double-decker, in this case number 20 in the Tilling fleet in London, a 1905 example.

# Milnes-Daimler

If we are to understand the impact the Milnes-Daimler double-decker made on the fledgling motor bus industry we must look back briefly to the transport scene at the beginning of the century. In the towns, horse buses and trams and growing numbers of electric trams carried the passengers, with the railway companies catering for longer distances. Although the motor car was becoming a more familiar sight, legislation and inexperience slowed the progress of the motor bus. There had been steam and battery-electric omnibuses, and there would be more, but early petrol-driven buses were often crude and cumbersome and did little to encourage widespread interest.

The Germans and the French played important parts in the early history of the motor car and the Daimler name is a particularly significant one. Gottlieb Daimler had developed his first motor car in 1885 and a few years later the Daimler patent rights for Britain were bought by the young engineer Frederick Simms, who in 1893 formed the Daimler Motor Syndicate Ltd, which in 1896 as the Daimler Motor Company Limited commenced production of motor cars in Coventry.

Enter G. F. Milnes & Co, the respected tramcar builders. The Milnes company had been re-formed in 1898 with German finance to cope with the high demand for electric tramcars. The company soon looked at the new internal combustion engine and Milnes marketed a German-built lorry from 1901 under an agreement with the manufacturers, Motorfahrzeug und Motorfabrik AG of Marienfelde. This firm was taken over in 1902 by Daimler Motoren Gesselschaft of Cannstatt and later in 1902 Daimler appointed Milnes as agents for its products.

Thus Milnes-Daimler Ltd was born and backed by the reputation of the German concern produced its first 16hp buses, which inaugurated two of the most notable early services. On 12 April 1903 four 14-seat Milnes-Daimlers were used to inaugurate the very first municipal motor bus service in Britain, at Eastbourne. Just four months later, on 17 August, the Great Western Railway used two 22-seat Milnes-Daimler wagonettes on a service from Helston to the Lizard, in Cornwall. The GWR buses had been bought in June by the Lynton & Barnstaple Railway for a service from Ilfracombe to Blackwood Station, but following problems (including 'speeding above 8mph') they were quickly resold. The Milnes-Daimlers proved satisfactory for GWR ordered 30 more in 1904 and in its steadily growing bus fleet had over 100 Milnes-Daimlers by 1908.

In February 1904 Milnes-Daimler introduced its 24hp double-decker at the Crystal Palace Motor Car Show — a purpose-built bus which was an instant success. The simple layout of the Milnes body set a pattern that remained largely unaltered for 15 years, with the engine mounted in front of the driver, who sat in the open under a canopy, and a simple open-top body with seats for 34 (18/16); the open platform and staircase were at the rear. The overall length was 16ft 3.5in (4.96m) and width was 6ft 6in (1.98m).

The 24hp Daimler engine drove through a constant mesh gearbox. At first the final drive was by chains but soon a differential type back axle was adopted. Although many of the early motor buses had wooden artillery-style spoked wheels the Milnes-Daimler had cast steel wheels.

The specification sounds basic today but when the Milnes-Daimler first appeared it represented a tremendous advance and operators were quick to appreciate its worth.

Then as now the London bus business was regarded by manufacturers as important and prestigious and early customers included two old-established horse bus operators, Thomas Tilling and Birch Brothers, each of whom started motor bus operation with Milnes-Daimlers in 1904.

The year 1904 closed with only 17 motor buses in London service, five of which were Milnes-Daimlers, but production at the Tottenham Court Road works in London increased to meet growing orders and a year later more than 80 were in service. Many of these buses were owned by a new and important face on the London scene, an operator with no horse bus experience — the London Motor Omnibus Co Ltd, using the name Vanguard initially as a route name but eventually as a fleetname.

Vanguard services started on 27 March 1905 with five Milnes-Daimlers and the company was astute enough to obtain priority on Milnes-Daimler deliveries. This caused the giant London General undertaking, still reluctantly developing its motor bus services, to switch to De Dions after a batch of Milnes-Daimlers in May 1905. The French-built De Dion was another of the Continental makes that dominated the London bus scene in the early years of the century and it was favoured by London General for some years before the company turned to the British-made Wolseley. More popular than the De Dion was the German Büssing built under licence as the Straker-Squire and favoured by the third main force in the London business, the London Road Car company. In May 1906 of over 400 motor buses in service in London 175 were Milnes-Daimlers followed by 101 Straker-

This 1905 photograph gives some idea of the world into which the Milnes-Daimler was born. This was one of five 25hp Milnes-Daimlers bought in 1905 by Bath Electric Tramways, fitted with Dodson 32-seat bodies. Seen at Wells Hill, Radstock, on the Bath–Midsomer Norton route.

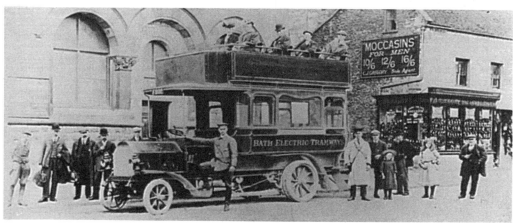

Another Bath Milnes-Daimler, registered FB 02, was the second (heavy) motor vehicle to be licensed in Bath, in August 1905, and the first motor bus for the Bath company. It is seen outside the town hall at Midsomer Norton, ready to return to Bath.

Squires, 52 De Dions, 27 Durkopps, 14 Scott-Stirlings, 13 Brillies, 12 Leylands, 7 Orions and 11 Clarkson steamers.

Milnes-Daimler's success in the motor bus market happened at the right time, for the Milnes tramway business went into liquidation because of a glut of manufacturers.

The motor bus was going through a period of fast and frequent development as manufacturers and operators came to grips with the new problems it created. The London motor bus population in the years 1903-1908 graphically illustrates the changes, rising from just 31 in 1903, passing 100 in 1906 and reaching over 1,000 in 1908. The Milnes-Daimler represented roughly one-third of this total in its peak year of 1907 but the Straker-Squire went on to pass the Milnes-Daimler that same year, reaching its peak in 1908.

The Milnes-Daimler was not just a London bus, although much of the motor bus activity of the early years was centred on the Metropolis. Milnes-Daimler double-deckers could also be found at several places on the south coast of England, and with the Great Western Railway, the London & North Western Railway and the Lancashire & Yorkshire Railway. With the London buses the total number of Milnes-Daimler buses in service in Britain in 1907 was 600; there were also some 300 Milnes-Daimler commercials working around the country.

Vanguard, however, is the name most closely associated with the Milnes-Daimler — and not just in London. In 1905 the company started an ambitious long-distance service between London and Brighton using Milnes-Daimler double-deckers, but a fatal crash on Handcross Hill in 1906 did little for public confidence and is reckoned to have set back the development of rural and inter-urban buses for several years. Nevertheless, Vanguard's London fleet went from strength to strength backed by an enthusiastic and far-sighted management. At a time when mechanical problems were rife, even on the comparatively reliable Milnes-Daimlers, Vanguard employed a team of travelling mechanics whose task was to go to the aid of the first reported breakdown in the morning and then travel on the service until another breakdown was encountered. The drivers had to act as engineers as well, for oil had to be pumped to the engine sump from a glass bottle on the dashboard.

Milnes-Daimler steadily improved the specification of the double-decker, with a longer version — 19ft 6in (5.94m) — in 1905 and an even longer 28hp version —

19ft 11in (6.07m) — in 1907. *Commercial Motor* was moved at the time to hail the Milnes-Daimler as 'a splendid example of high class workmanship'.

The reign of the Milnes-Daimler was brief but significant and it was largely overtaken by events. The Vanguard company turned to Thornycrofts and in 1906 had opened its Motor Omnibus Construction company at Walthamstow to build its own chassis. Then on 1 July 1908 the three main motor bus operators in London, General, Road Car and Vanguard, decided to cut their growing losses and amalgamated as the new London General. At the time these three fleets operated 885 of the 1,066 motor buses in London, and of these Vanguard had by far the biggest fleet. Straker-Squires dominated the initial fleet, 356 of them, but Milnes-Daimlers were not far behind with 312. In many ways this was the end of the road for Milnes-Daimler for as we shall see the new combine rapidly developed in its own standard motor buses which were to represent as great an advance in the evolution of the bus as the Milnes-Daimler had been in 1904.

In addition to its commercial vehicle

interests the Milnes-Daimler company had also agreed to act as agents for German Mercedes (Daimler) cars, and this side of the business was becoming increasingly important. This, combined with the disappearance of Vanguard and the increasing competition from other motor bus manufacturers, contributed towards the decline of the commercial vehicle business. The onset of World War 1 was the final straw for a company relying on German supplies. The firm — which in 1912 had been renamed Milnes-Daimler-Mercedes Ltd — was wound up in 1916, but was not finally dissolved for another six years. An inauspicious end for an important company.

One Milnes-Daimler has survived, registered D 1959, and new in 1905 to the Brighton, Hove & Preston United Omnibus company. It made an appearance, with replica body to recall its former glory, at the 1976 HCVC London to Brighton Run, but was shipped off to a new home in the United States. Even that brief glimpse of the first of the classic buses was a reminder of the important part it had once played at the dawn of the motor era.

One of the large Milnes-Daimler fleet built up by the London Motor Omnibus Company — Vanguard — attracts an interested crowd as it prepares to set off from London on its long-distance run to Brighton in August 1905.

*Right:* The smartly turned-out conductor leans proudly on the mudguard of this 1905 Milnes-Daimler 20hp in the Tilling fleet. The rugged simplicity of the design is well illustrated.

8

London General also tried a small batch of Milnes-Daimlers in its early motorised fleet, but switched to De Dions after Vanguard obtained a priority on deliveries.

The beautiful replica body on D1959, the 1904 Milnes-Daimler 28hp preserved in Brighton Hove & Preston United livery, and now in the United States.

*Right:* Away from its normal habitat, but unmistakably a London General B type. B4973, a 1919 bus, seen on route 84 from rural Golders Green to St Albans.

London General was slow to appreciate the potential of the motor bus. As Britain's largest horse bus operator, the prospect of wholesale conversion to motor buses was a daunting one, and there were several strong anti-bus factions to contend with. As late as 1910 the general manager of London County Council Tramways prophesied that 'in ten years' time there will not be a motor bus outside a museum'. He was wrong, of course, but progress was slow in the first decade of this century, and fast-growing motor bus fleets like Vanguard and Road Car represented a serious challenge to London General. The amalgamation of General, Road Car and Vanguard in 1908 strengthened the new General's hand, and its chief engineer, Frank Searle, was to play an important part in the development of the company and indeed of the motor bus.

Searle was trained as a locomotive engineer, and had become involved in the motor bus business as a consultant, also importing the French Lacoste-Battman chassis. He joined the London & District Motorbus Co Ltd (the Arrow fleet, associated with the Vanguard company), but in 1907, at the age of 33, was appointed superintendent of General's Mortlake garage. Within three months he was moved to General's main Dollis Hill garage where he found 28 different chassis types among the 70 motor buses — which were still housed alongside 300 horses. His first move was to allocate buses to garages by chassis type. He soon became General's chief motor engineer and when the newly-amalgamated London General proposed an order for 200 Wolseleys Searle suggested that the company should make its own buses.

He used the former Motor Omnibus Construction Works of the Vanguard company at Blackhorse Lane, Walthamstow, and set about combining the best elements of the existing General buses — 'we cribbed shamelessly', he later wrote — to produce the X type in August 1909, the 'Daimler-Wolseley-Straker' as his critics dubbed it. The same month the Commissioner of the Metropolitan Police, who for so long stifled the natural development of the London bus, introduced new and almost impossible restrictive legislation governing the size and weight of new buses. The X type, which ran to 61 vehicles, gave Searle the experience he needed, and a new design within the new limits appeared in October 1910. This was the first B type.

In concept the B type was similar to other contemporary buses, but ingenious design had produced a light yet sturdy machine. The new four-cylinder side-valve petrol engine of around 5.3 litres produced 25hp at 800rpm,

and was noted for its good torque; it could attain speeds of up to 35mph in spite of the 12mph legal maximum! The rear axle was worm-driven, and there was a cone clutch and a four-speed 'silent' chain gearbox. The wheels were steel rather than wood and the chassis frame was ash with nickel steel flitch plates. The wheelbase was 12ft 10 5/8in (3.92m).

The body was 22ft.5in (6.87m) long and 6ft 11in (2.10m) wide, and was 12ft 5in (3.78m) from the ground at the highest point. There were seats for 34, 18 on wooden-slatted forward facing seats on the open top deck and 16 on upholstered inward-facing seats downstairs. Lighting was originally acetylene and oil lamps, and from 1912 electric. The bodies were built by London General at North Road, Olaf Street and Seagrave Road, and were also sub-contracted to famous London coachbuilders like Dodson and Hora, and even to the Motherwell firm of Hurst Nelson. Not all B types carried the standard body for in many cases earlier bodies were transferred from old chassis, including Arrol-Johnsons, Milnes-Daimlers and Straker-Squires.

In the words of J. B. Atkinson from his excellent monograph on the class *The London B type Motor Omnibus*, the B type was 'slow, simple, open to the elements, but above all reliable and known and depended upon by millions of Londoners for work and play'. And so it was, for the B type really opened up General's motor bus empire.

With eight others, B1 started on the new route 25 from Victoria to Old Ford in October 1910, and by the end of the year 33 Bs were in service. A year later that figure had jumped to over 700, and in 1912 no fewer than 1,400 chassis were built — roughly 28 a week, a figure that some modern manufacturers would regard with envy. The massive injection of new B types allowed General to start nearly 50 new motor bus services and open eight new garages.

In 1912 General was acquired by the Underground Electric Railways Group, as a result of which the company's operating area was allowed to grow. Another consequence of the take-over was the creation of the Associated Equipment Company (AEC) as a separate entity to build and market the Walthamstow-built chassis.

Meanwhile Frank Searle was still active. He had been persuaded in 1911 to join the Daimler company, and in 1912 developed the Daimler CC type, a bus that was not dissimiliar to the B type. In a roundabout way the Daimler CC led to closer ties between AEC and Daimler as we shall see in the chapter on the Daimler COG5 and COG6.

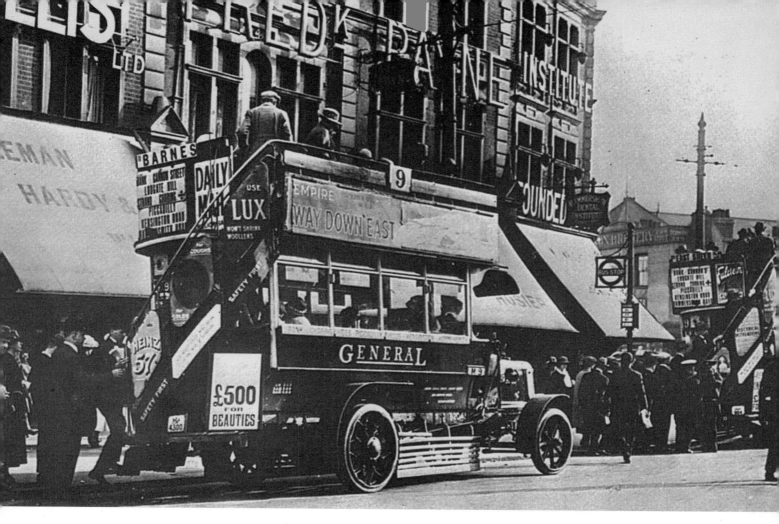

Two B types in more familiar
surroundings — loading at
Hammersmith in 1921 on the
9 route.

Back to the B type and increasing numbers were taking to the London streets. Most, but not all, were standard double-deckers; there were also B type charabancs, single-deck buses and even lorries and parcel vans. And not all the double-deckers were in General red, for eventually roughly one in every ten B types wore the colours of a General associated fleet, and carried fleetnames like Associated, Metropolitan, MET, Central and Southern.

By 1914 and the start of World War I the General fleet had grown to 3,100 motor buses, of which more than 2,700 were Bs. In the four years from 1910, when the B had first appeared, the General network had grown from 23 motor bus services to 109.

The value of the motor vehicle in a war was soon appreciated in 1914 and buses were requisitioned for use in Europe, as troop carriers moving men into line and between sectors, and as ambulances and wireless vehicles. Nearly 1,000 B types, plus many Daimlers, were employed on war service, while at home the General fleet total fell to such a degree that older X types and De Dions were relicensed. From 1915 General was able to repurchase B types from the War Department, and many re-entered London service. A few new B types were built during

the war, but AEC was fully occupied building more than 10,000 Y type trucks.

The last B types were built in 1919, the same year its successor the K type appeared. The K type was bigger, with 46 seats, and the driver sat beside rather than behind the engine. But the B was far from dead. A new single-deck body was developed and mounted on B chassis, and B types appeared in London's country, with the National and East Surrey fleets.

Although the new K and S types appeared in increasing numbers, the B type still represented more than half the General fleet in 1921. From the mid-1920s the Bs were withdrawn fairly rapidly. Some were scrapped but some were sold for further service all over Britain. The last General B type double-decker ran in service late in 1926, and the single-deckers lasted until June 1927. That was not the end, though, for General's B type box vans lasted until 1928, trainers until 1930, and there were even two B type lorries which survived to 1934, by which time the London Passenger Transport Board had been formed.

The B type was not exclusively a London bus. In the early days new B types went to United Auto and Rotherham Corporation, and after World War I some of the buses not

13

required by General were sold on their return from Europe. When withdrawals first started the B types were snatched up eagerly, but it was by then an 'old' bus in an era of short lives, and faster, pneumatic-tyred vehicles had a greater appeal.

Over the years there were several minor improvements to the B, most notably more powerful engines developing up to 45hp. The fact that the B enjoyed a lifespan of 16 years is a tribute to the soundness of Frank Searle's original concept.

We can still see B types today, for there are four complete vehicles and one chassis preserved. The most famous are B43 and B340, which are still on view in London. Both buses were built in 1911 and saw war

service from 1914, B43 in France and B340 at home. B43, nicknamed Ole Bill after the famous Bairnsfather cartoon character, was presented to the Auxiliary Omnibus Company's Old Comrades Association, and in 1970 was driven to its present resting place at the Imperial War Museum at Lambeth. B340 lasted in service until 1924, and was sent to Vancouver in 1936 for the Golden Jubilee celebrations there. In 1960 it went on show at the new Museum of British Transport at Clapham, moving eventually to Syon Park and ultimately to Covent Garden. One of the other preserved B types, B214, is again a 1911 bus, and is now preserved with a double-deck body.

**Piccadilly by night — or early morning to judge from the station clock — and 1911-built B185 on the 94 night service early in its life.**

While most of London General's Bs were double-deckers, there were a number which carried single-deck bodies at some time. B1357 was a 1912 charabanc for private hire work, although it was requisitioned for war work, and, when repurchased, received a standard double-deck body.

In 1920 B4900, built the previous year as a double-decker, received this prototype 26-seat single-deck body, based on the body fitted to contemporary K type single-deckers. A further 74 similar B type buses were built in 1921.

15

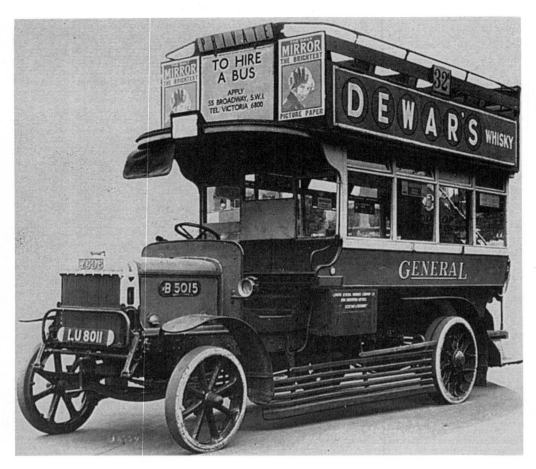

Representing the ultimate B type, B5015 was a 1919 example which was kept in pristine condition for private hire work. (It is interesting that some 60 years later, Londoners are still being exhorted to hire a bus from 55 Broadway in similar terms). This bus survived on driver training duties, at least until 1927.

*Right:* The unmistakable shape of a Leyland PLSC3 Lion — a 1928 United Counties example, seen in Kettering in the late 1930s.

The famous B43, 'Ole Bill', was presented by LGOC to the Auxiliary Omnibus Companies Old Comrades Association, and now resides in the Imperial War Museum. A 1911 bus, it is seen here in 1950 en route between Sutton and Old Kent Road garages.

# Leyland Lion PLSC

The fact that Leyland is today at the heart of Britain's indigenous motor industry is due in no small measure to the Leyland PLSC Lion. Leyland's roots were in the Lancashire Steam Motor Co Ltd, founded in 1896 to build steam vehicles. From 1904 the firm built an increasing number of petrol-engined vehicles, including buses for service in London and Manchester which were labelled 'Leyland'. In 1907 the company became Leyland Motors Ltd, and rapidly became an important supplier to home and overseas fleets with a range of simple and reliable chassis suitable for goods or passenger bodywork — occasionally both as bodies were switched to cater for the more profitable work of the moment.

During World War I Leyland built almost 6,000 vehicles for what became the Royal Air Force, and to safeguard its reputation after the war purchased and rebuilt several thousand for resale. In doing this the company created a financial crisis, further exaggerated by the depression of 1920 and a drop in commercial vehicle prices. Leyland cut prices but even this drastic action almost came too late, for years of poor management had caught up with what had started as a promising company.

As we know, Leyland weathered the storm, and its passenger vehicle business and its new L range of 1925 did much to improve financial viability.

The L range was designed from the outset to be used as passenger vehicles. The old concept of common chassis for buses and lorries was now largely laid to rest — at least by Leyland. And this was good news for bus passengers, for it heralded a welcome move towards lower frame heights and greater sophistication. These added up to easier passenger access and a more comfortable ride, and in many ways represented the birth of the bus as a really serious competitor for tramcars and railways.

Leyland was not the first to introduce a low-frame bus chassis range, but it is fair to describe the L models as the most successful and best-remembered. The five models were the Leopard, Leviathan, Leveret, Lioness and Lion. The Leopard was a long, forward control single-decker, but only two were built. The Leviathan was a double-decker, though outside London the market was small, and less than 100 were built. The Leveret was a small normal control model and the Lioness an imposing full-size normal control model, and both sold in small numbers. The star of the range was undoubtedly the Lion.

Here was a low-built single-deck chassis with a wheelbase of 14ft 6in (4.41m), suitable for bodies up to 25ft (7.62m) long. The engine was an overhead-valve four-cylinder 5.1-litre petrol unit and a four-speed sliding mesh gearbox was fitted. The Lion had a double-reduction rear axle which created the distinctive whine which characterised the progress of every PLSC.

The original Lion of 1925 was classified LSC1, with the better-known PLSC1 designation for chassis with pneumatic tyres. In fact it seems unlikely that any ran on anything but pneumatics.

With a frame almost 1ft (30cm) lower than previous Leyland models the Lion was an instant success, selling at £870 for the chassis, or £1,420 complete with Leyland 31-seat body. Leyland had built charabanc and bus bodies from an early stage, and its simple outright wooden framed body for the PLSC Lion was a classic and functional design.

In 1926 the PLSC3 'Long Lion' was introduced alongside the PLSC1, with a 16ft 5in (5m) wheelbase, suitable for 26ft (7.92m) bodies seating up to 35. The PLSC3 continued the PLSC1's success, but things were happening quickly in the late 1920s, as manufacturers and operators really got to grips with the motor bus. The PLSC3 Lion only lasted three years on the Leyland model list before it was succeeded by the LT1 Lion, which had much in common with the successful new Tiger and Titan models, but which had a new four-cylinder engine. Progress overtook the PLSC range, advanced and acceptable when it was new, but crude and outdated in comparison with some of the smoother and more refined chassis that took over its role at the end of the decade. Nonetheless. PLSC Lions soldiered on all over Britain, and many moved on to new homes after being edged out by their six cylinder successors.

The most remarkable of the long-lived Lions survived in Jersey, with Jersey Motor Transport, until the 1960s. This brought them into the preservation era, and meant that several ex-JMT Lions could be rescued and returned to the mainland for restoration.

More than 2,500 PLSC Lions were built in the model's four-year lifespan, and Leyland bodies were fitted to a large proportion of these. Fortunately, 13 Lions are preserved today, to allow us to sample the sights and sounds of yesterday. Most originally hailed from the north of England, from Lancashire and Yorkshire — traditionally Leyland strongholds — although for some Lions it represents a return to the north after spending most of their lives basking in the Jersey sun.

On private hire duties at Scarborough in July 1934, a 1927 PLSC1 Lion of Grey-de-Luxe Coaches, Hull.

In Scotland, Alexanders built up a sizeable fleet of PLSC Lions. This 1927 PLSC3 with Leyland body is seen in Glasgow when new.

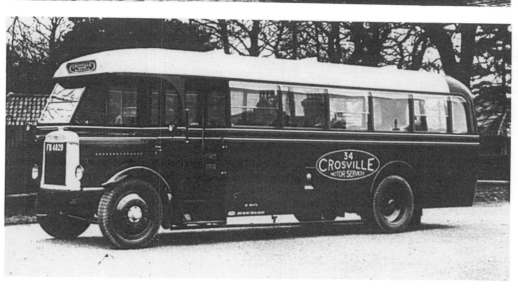

Although the PLSC Lions were quickly rendered out-of-date by the rapid developments in bus chassis design in the 1920s, some operators chose to rebody them. This 1928 Crosville bus (*left*), rebodied by Eastern Counties in 1934, was originally a bonneted Lioness PLC1, but was rebuilt as a forward-control PLSC on rebodying. The standard Crosville PLSC1/Leyland (*above*) was new in 1927.

The Leyland "Lion."

Leyland Motors, Ltd., specialise in their comfortable and speedy Leyland passenger models, the last words in design and finish. Many original and appealing features, including a side-opening gear box which permits of thorough inspection of the gears, are embodied in the classic design, and the coachwork is unsurpassable. The power units are most powerful and sweet in running. The double-reduction Leyland axle with spiral bevel and double helical spur gears is the most modern of its kind and is particularly quiet in running.

*The Leyland "Lion"—A 31-Seater Single-Deck Model.*

A large demand exists for these vehicles amongst Corporations and concerns owning public motor services at home and abroad. Extremely popular is the Leyland "Lion" 31-seater single-deck model, with a front entrance type body and enclosed driving position alongside the engine on the off-side. Its graceful body has a low-load line, the interior is beautifully finished, and the whole vehicle presents a most striking appearance.

*Far left:* An extract from 'The Electric Railway & Tramway Journal' of May 1926 describes the Lion in glowing terms.

For the filming of 'The Prime of Miss Jean Brodie' in 1968, this 1928 ex-Jersey PLSC1 (*left and below, centre*) received Edinburgh Corporation livery and an appropriate registration.

*Right:* Southdown 1930 all-Leyland Titan TD1s in the bodyshops at Portslade in 1937, showing the distinctive piano-front outline. Southdown accumulated 143 TD1s between 1929-32.

Two preserved PLSCs. *Below left:* Photographed in Jersey Motor Transport livery, this 1927 PLSC3 is now preserved in the livery of its original owner, Blythe & Berwick, of Bradford. It is seen on an early rally, at Leyland Motors in 1958. *Below:* An immaculate ex-Ribble 1927 PLSC1 at the Chester Transport centenary cavalcade in 1979.

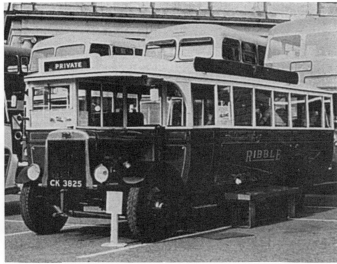

# Leyland Titan TD1

PRIVATE
SOUTHDOWN
UF 5654

While pneumatic tyres and low frames were encouraging even wider acceptance of the single-deck bus in the 1920s, the double-decker had barely advanced beyond the stage reached by the Milnes-Daimler and London General B type in the days before World War I. In fact the double-decker was still very much a London animal, and those double-deckers which could be found in other towns and cities in Britain were very much to London designs. Manufacturers were astute enough to build to London standards, and that did not just mean London General, for from 1922 a host of small independents challenged General's monopoly, and forced the development of the double-decker a step further — they might have taken it even further if the Metropolitan Police had not stunted natural progress.

General's answer to the better buses of the independents was the AEC NS of 1923, designed by LGOC and AEC with a low frame, pneumatic tyres and a covered top. The Metropolitan Police regulations, which still governed the design of London's buses, delayed the appearance of top-covered NSs in service until 1925, and pneumatic-tyred NSs until 1928. Covered-top double-deckers were not new outside London, but the acceptance of pneumatics depended heavily on their continued development — first on lighter-weight then on full size single-deckers, and from 1926 on the six-wheel double-deckers that enjoyed a vogue with some operators; at the time four-wheel single-deckers were restricted to around 25ft (7.62m) long, while six-wheelers could be up to 30ft (9.14m) long, offering several advantages, the most practical for many operators being increased seating capacity.

Leyland's double-deck range was making less spectacular progress than the equivalent single-deck range in the mid-1920s. The double-decker in the 1925 range, the Leviathan, like the London NS was produced in open and covered-top styles, on solid tyres and on pneumatics. Only 93 Leviathans were built in its two-year model life, and its replacement could hardly have been more of a contrast. The Leyland Titan TD1 was the undoubted hit of the 1927 Olympia Commercial Motor Show. It was modern where the Leviathan was archaic, and sleek whereas the latter was high-built and clumsy. It was the rebirth of the double-decker and in many ways the birth of the modern bus. Its main mechanical advance was the adoption of a six-cylinder engine, a 6.8-litre overhead camshaft petrol unit, which was driven through a four-speed sliding mesh gearbox. The equivalent single-deck model was the Tiger TS1.

The Titan came complete with lowbridge Leyland-built body, with seats for 48 passengers. The upper deck seating, with a sunken offside gangway, brought the overall height down to just 13ft (3.96m) — around 2ft-3ft (60cm-90cm) lower than previous covered-top double-deckers. The body styling had a smoothness of line that broke away from the essentially square shapes of other bodies, with their horse bus and tramcar origins and ornately-panelled liveries.

The upper deck projected above the enclosed driver's cab, and traced a line back to the upper deck front windows with a slight step, the distinctive 'piano front' outline. The rear staircase was open. A complete Titan weighed about 5.75 tons — the chassis was 3.5 tons, the body 2.25 tons.

The lowbridge body was standard until 1930, when the 14ft (4.26m) Hybridge version appeared with normal seating on both decks for 51 passengers. By 1929 most Titans were fitted with fully-enclosed staircases, although the open staircase was available until 1932, and some operators continued to specify them. Some operators, notably Southdown, continued to fit open-top bodies to their Titans, and Titans for the independent operators in London were restricted by the Metropolitan Police regulations, and required an open cab for the driver until 1929.

The Titan did much to restore confidence in the double-decker for inter-urban and rural work, for the spectre of the 1906 Handcross Hill accident lingered on. It was readily recognised as the forerunner of a new breed of bus, and was ordered in large numbers by the growing fleets of the day.

Municipal fleets were obvious Titan customers. Manchester used lowbridge TD1s for its controversial conversion of the single-deck 53 tram route to motor bus operation — the start of the end for Manchester's trams; Glasgow Corporation built up a fleet of 273 TD1s between 1928 and 1931.

Company operators flocked in with their orders; in its first 18 months on the market more than 1,400 Tigers and Titans were ordered; TD1s helped the outward expansion of still-familiar names like Alexanders, Ribble and Southdown. The London 'pirate' fleets recognised the Titan's potential, and when the London Passenger Transport Board took them over in the 1930s, 193 buses joined its appropriately-coded TD class.

Leyland's publicity men coined a number of well-remembered slogans for the Titan. 'When you bury a tram,' ran a famous one, 'mark the spot with a Titan.' And equally true was the advertising description of the Titan as 'the lowest bus with the highest sales'.

But for an unsolicited testimonial the

words of A. F. R. Carling, one-time general manager of the Southdown company, are worth recalling. Describing the TD1 as the 'paragon of vehicle virtues', he said that it offered 'if not quite the capacity and durability of the tramcar, certainly something much nearer them than anything available before, and it combined these advantages with the greater comfort and far greater mobility of the bus.'

Buses like the Titan helped instil confidence in the travelling public, and the raising of the speed limit for buses on pneumatics from 12 to 20mph in 1928 encouraged the wider use of buses and severely challenged the dominant positions held by tramways and railways on urban and inter-urban transport.

The TD1 was succeeded in 1931 by the TD2, with a 7.6 litre engine, by which time around 2,400 TD1s had been built. Of these, nine have been preserved, including WH1553, the well-known ex-Bolton Corporation example from 1929. This had been set aside by Leyland in 1956 for a projected company museum, but a change in policy led Leyland to pass it into the hands of the Lincolnshire Vintage Vehicle Society on permanent loan in 1965. In 1970 WH1553's

restoration was complete, and it was given its first public airing at the London to Brighton Run of the HCVC. I was fortunate to travel down with WH on that day, a welcome opportunity to sample a TD1 in original condition. The ride was quiet and smooth, unremarkable perhaps by modern standards, but it is important to remember the sensation the Titan created more than 50 years ago, pioneering so many of the features we now take for granted.

The TD1 Titan was the first of a distinguished line of buses to carry the name. It directly fathered the TD series which were in production from 1927 to 1942, with successive improvements culminating in the TD7 of 1939-42. The Titan name reappeared in 1946 with the PD1 model and ran through to 1969 with the bigger-engined PD2 and PD3 variants. The name made yet another reappearance in 1977 on Leyland's 'new generation' B15 double-decker. Although 50 years separate the TD1 from the new TN15 Titan, a 1920s advertising slogan seems particularly appropriate even today: 'The Titan, the bus for tomorrow — today.'

A well-known photograph, but one which dramatically illustrates the advance in bus design represented by the Titan TD1. The high-built, cumbersome-looking bus was a 1926 Crosville Leyland Leviathan LSP1, and behind it, only one year younger (!), heralding the birth of the modern double-decker is a 1927 TD1 prototype.

Glasgow Corporation bought 273 TD1s between 1928 and 1931, and these views show two different 1928 examples and, in particular, the open rear staircase leading from the upper deck sunken offside gangway.

Another fine offical view (*left*) of a Titan TD1, in this case a 1929 example for Bradford. The body mouldings persuaded many operators to switch to simpler liveries than had previously been favoured; the style shown here, with three parallel bands of cream or white became standard in many fleets. Another Bradford TD1 is seen (*below*) in service in Lord Street, Huddersfield in 1937, behind two apparently camera-shy passengers and an airborne dog. The bodywork on this TD1 was actually built by Vickers, to Leyland design.

One of Manchester Corporation's famous TD1 Titans, with lowbridge Strachans 48-seat bodywork, used in 1930 for the conversion of the former 53 tram route. 243 is seen in Old Trafford.

*Two great achievements in Transport and Architecture*

Leyland

The TD1 and the Scott Monument in Edinburgh are hailed as 'great achievements' in this 1930 Leyland advertisement. The bus was one of 37 delivered in 1929 to SMT.

One of Southport Corporation's first Leylands was this 1930 Titan TD1, seen in Lord Street when new. The 51-seat lowbridge body was Leyland-built.

By contrast, this 1928 Lancashire United TD1 was looking rather down-at-heel when photographed at Atherton late in its life, in 1950.

Many TD1s were rebodied or rebuilt to extend their useful lives. This 1930 TD1 was new to Southdown in 1930, and can be seen in its original condition on page 21. In 1938 it passed to Western SMT with 22 of its brothers, and in 1946 was sold to Crosville, who fitted this new ECW 53-seat body in 1949. It lasted in this form until 1956, and is seen in Rhyl in the early 1950s.

An unusual rebodying was carried out in 1941 for Barton Transport, when this 1930 ex-Chatham & District TD1 received a stylish forward-entrance Duple 55-seat lowbridge body, with no hint of wartime restrictions in the design.

The Lincolnshire Vintage Vehicle Society's ex-Bolton TD1 of 1929, WH 1553, is a familiar sight at rallies throughout the country. These photographs were taken at Warwick in 1972.

*Right:* Two AEC Regals of Bath Tramways, against the imposing backdrop of Bath Abbey. They were new in 1937 with Eastern Coach Works bodies.

Titans compared. The LVVS ex-Bolton TD1 alongside one of the Leyland's prototype TN15 Titans, at the MIRA test track, in 1977.

# AEC Regal

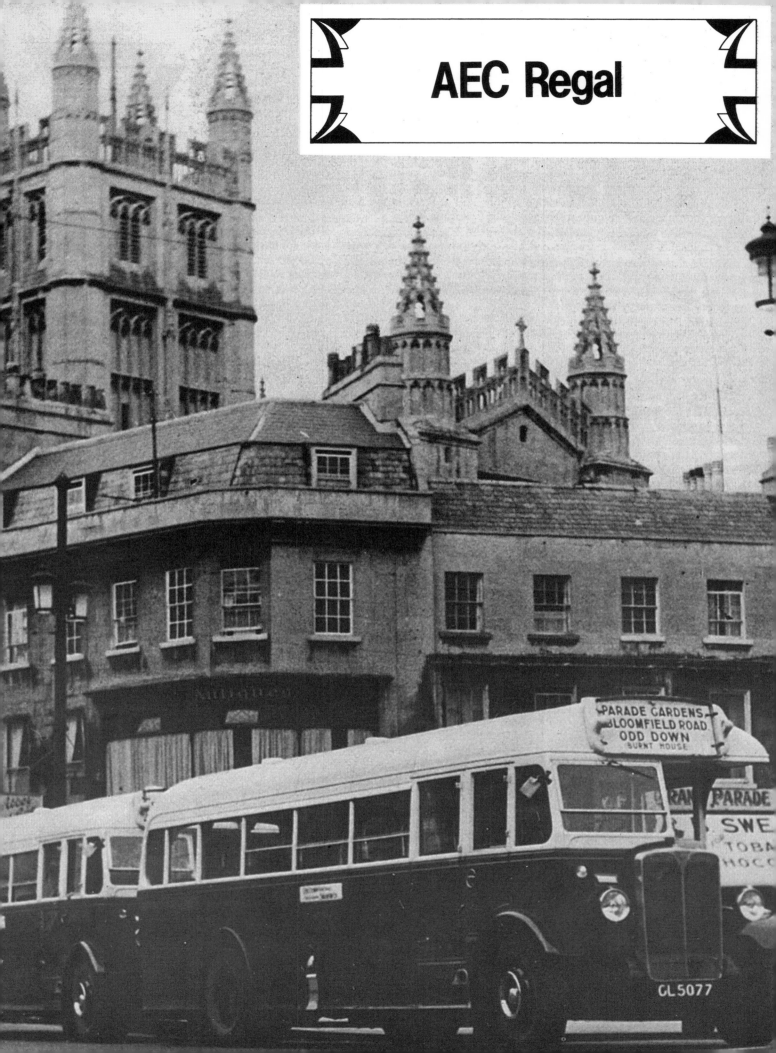

One man who left his mark on bus design in the 1930s, and whose influence lingered on long after that decade, was G. J. Rackham. He had started in the old Vanguard company at its Walthamstow works, and had a hand in the development of the London B type. He left what had become AEC in 1916 and six years later became chief engineer with the Yellow Coach and Truck company in Chicago. He was lured back to Britain in 1926 to become Leyland's chief engineer, and as such was largely responsible for the six-cylinder Tiger/Titan chassis range which did so much for the evolution of the motor bus, and which helped Leyland steal a march on its rivals.

AEC's close liaison with London General guaranteed a regular flow of bus business, but the company was anxious to sell its products on a very much wider scale and persuaded Rackham to join the company at its new Southall plant in 1928. His first stopgap move was to fit a six-cylinder engine into a chassis based on the ADC426, which was then christened the AEC Reliance. While the Reliance was enjoying a short and successful model life Rackham was working on a completely new range which would at least be the equal of Leyland's Tigers and Titans. The result was the appearance in 1929 of the AEC Regal and Regent.

The recipe was similar to Leyland's, and just as successful. The two models, single-deck Regal and double-deck Regent, were similar mechanically, with the 6.1 litre six-cylinder ohc petrol engine, a single-plate clutch and a sliding mesh gearbox. The Regal had 17ft (5.18m) wheelbase for bodies up to 26ft (7.92m) long, while the Regent was suitable for bodies up to 25ft (7.62m) long. Just as Leyland had introduced a six-wheel double-deck chassis, the Titanic, AEC introduced the Renown, which enjoyed a greater success, due largely to orders from London. The Regent double-decker was the largest seller — around 7,000 between 1929 and 1942 — but we have considered its contemporary, the Leyland Titan, and will look here at the single-deck Regal in more detail. The Regal/Regent/Renown range was an AEC venture, independent of London General, but General was quick to appreciate the potential of the new models. Although the first 12 Regal 662 models went to Plymouth Corporation, London General was not far behind, as an enthusiastic writer informed his readers in the very first issue of *The Omnibus Magazine* in January 1930:

'The LGOC have commenced the replacement of the single-deck Ks with the magnificent 30-seat single-deckers of class T, the AEC Regal chassis being used. This is fitted

with a six-cylinder engine of great liveliness, rated at 37.2hp and developing 48bhp at 1,000 and 95bhp at 2,500 revs per min. The acceleration and running speeds are good, and riding is very comfortable. A low frame level is achieved by off-setting the propeller shaft to the near side, so that the axle pot is under a seat. One or two excrescences still remain in the floor however. The lighting is of the excellent concealed type, being diffused through ceiling panels. Readers interested in these vehicles for themselves will find nearly 50 at work in the London area at the time of writing.'

Sales of the new range were spectacular. By the end of 1930 around 1,500 chassis, single-deck and double-deck, had been built.

A larger six-cylinder petrol engine, a 7.4 litre unit, appeared in Regals from 1932, but there were still operators who favoured four-cylinder engines, and a 5.1 litre unit was developed. This was fitted in a new chassis, designated by AEC the Regal 4 (model 642) unlike Leyland who chose to retain the Lion name for its four-cylinder models.

The oil engine made its appearance in AEC chassis experimentally in 1930, and the 8.8 litre AEC-Ricardo engine was available in all models from 1932. The same year the Daimler preselective gearbox was offered as an option, and two years later AEC developed its own version.

Another oil engine, the 7.7 litre unit, was introduced in 1934, and quickly became a popular choice in Regals and Regents. A less popular choice was the 6.6-litre 'light six' engine introduced in 1935, and fitted to a new lightweight model the Regal Mk II; just over 100 were built. Although AEC engines were standard, some fleets, notably Huddersfield Corporation, specified the Gardner 6LW to cope with its notorious hills. The Gardner-engined Regals and Regents featured a projecting front radiator to cope with the greater length of the 6LW unit.

The Regal was an adaptable chassis, and could be found on stage carriage, long-distance and touring work. Fleets of all sizes included Regals, and together with the Leyland Tiger could be seen in all parts of Britain as the most universally popular full-size single-deck chassis of the 1930s.

London General and its associates had a large Regal fleet, and when the London Passenger Transport Board was formed in 1933 it inherited 373 Regals in its T class, of which more than 300 were coaches. London Transport's first new T class vehicles were also coaches, 50 Weymann-bodied 30-seat Regals received in 1936. Two years later came the famous London 10T10 coaches,

266 Regals with 8.8 litre engines and pre-selective gearboxes, which maintained Green Line services before and after World War II.

In 1963 Alan Townsin, then editor of *Buses Illustrated*, a former AEC employee and a great AEC enthusiast, rode from London to Brighton and back on the preserved Green Line Regal T219.

This was one of 100 similar 30-seat coaches with bodies by three different builders supplied in 1930/31 for the new but rapidly expanding Green Line fleet associated with London General. The preserved coach was at the time resident in the Museum of British Transport of Clapham, London, but since then has been on view at Syon Park and is now at Covent Garden.

The petrol-engined coach has a Duple-built body and Alan Townsin eagerly took the opportunity to sample it on what was the second of the HCVC's London to Brighton runs. He wrote in *Buses Illustrated*:

'The Regal in those days had a six-cylinder overhead-camshaft petrol engine as standard. This was produced in two cylinder bore sizes, 100mm and 110mm, which with a stroke dimension of 130mm gave alternative capacities of 6.1 and 7.4 litres respectively. The maximum power output varied, depend-ing on carburettor and cylinder head variants, but could reach 120bhp with the larger unit and does not seem to have been less than 90bhp for any standard version of the smaller unit. With unladen weights of around 6 tons (appreciably less for some single-decker buses and not much more for many of the corresponding early Regent double-deckers) quite a good performance was produced.

'There is no need to qualify this by saying "by the standards of the time", for the power:weight ratios were quite equal to those commonly found on 1963 public service vehicles. A typical early Regal with 30 passengers, driver and conductor would turn the scales at about 8½ tons gross. If it had the 120bhp 'high power' head version of the 110m-bore engine it had a power:weight ratio of 14.1bhp per ton. A new AEC Reliance 590 36ft coach can be expected to weigh about 11 tons gross with, say, 49 passengers, and with the 153bhp engine would have a power:weight ratio of 13.9bhp per ton. So much for the common notion that all old buses were slow chuggers.

'Even more surprising to many people nowadays is the fact that the petrol engine of the standard 1929-32 Regal had a wider speed range than most 1963 diesels. It would

run up to 2,500rpm quite happily and many regular drivers would not normally change up until about 2,000rpm were reached, unless deliberately dawdling. This was undoubtedly the best technique for getting a move on.'

Regal production continued at a steady level until the outbreak of war in 1939. The cessation of 'non-essential' coach work and the need to concentrate on higher-capacity double-deckers brought the story of the prewar Regal to a halt after roughly 3,500 chassis had been built in a decade.

The Regal, largely in its prewar form, returned in 1945 when AEC's postwar range appeared. Most manufacturers concentrated on mechanically unadventurous models to satisfy vehicle-hungry operators, and the Regal Mk I of the 1945-47 era was very much to a prewar specification, with crash gearbox and 7.7 litre engine. Around 1,500 were built, in many cases for company operators, and it was succeeded by the Regal Mk III 0962, a more advanced chassis which owed much to the Regent Mk III double-decker and, in turn, to the London RT design of 1938. The initial model had the big 9.6 litre engine and preselective gearbox of the Regent Mk III, but demand for a smaller engine and more basic transmission produced the 0682 version, with the faithful 7.7 litre engine and a crash gearbox option on models with both engines.

Around 2,200 Regal IIIs were built, including roughly 600 with the 7.7 litre engine. They lost ground only when the underfloor-engined Regal Mk IV appeared in 1950 and this prompted a large-scale switch to these larger-capacity vehicles. The Regal Mk III continued in the model lists until 1957, but sales dwindled fast, particularly after 1954.

The Regal Mk IV was itself quickly succeeded on the home market by the lighter-weight, smaller-engined Reliance, but the Regal family survived for many years as a sturdy export model.

As a home market model, though, the Regal enjoyed a long life and an excellent reputation. Over 7,000 of the front-engined Regals were built including 3,500 prewar models, and the intervention of World War II meant that many were required to remain in service long after they would normally have been honourably retired. I recall some elderly Regals of 1935 vintage still in service with Scottish Omnibuses well into the 1960s, albeit disguised under full-fronted Burlingham Seagull bodies built halfway through their long lives. Scottish Omnibuses' predecessor, SMT, had built up a sizeable Regal fleet in the period 1931-40, unlike its SMT group brothers who preferred successive

models of the Leyland Tiger. SMT also bought Tigers before the war, but stuck to the Regal in postwar days, and withdrew its Tigers prematurely — by Scottish standards anyway.

And this was the situation with many operators. They bought Regals and came back for more. Regals performed well on all types of duty, although they were most often found on long-distance and coaching duties with company and independent fleets. Municipal Regals were less familiar. More than three quarters of London's T class Regals were coaches, although the last Ts, bought in the early postwar years, were Regal Mk I and Regal Mk III service buses, bringing the highest fleet number to T798.

Eleven prewar Regals are preserved, the oldest being a 1929 former London General bus. Newer preserved Regals include six Regal Mk Is and no less than 28 Regal Mk IIIs.

AEC advertising in the 1930s made a great deal of the AEC badge, as on this 1932 example featuring an early Regal (chassis 662015), supplied to the LMS Railway in 1930, with Harrington 21-seat coach body.

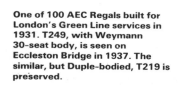

This AEC Regal 4 with Burlingham
28-seat body began life in 1933,
briefly as a demonstrator and
then joining the Isle of Man Road
Services fleet. It lasted in service
until 1955, and was stored until
1961 (*see inset*), when it became
a henhouse.

One of 100 AEC Regals built for
London's Green Line services in
1931. T249, with Weymann
30-seat body, is seen on
Eccleston Bridge in 1937. The
similar, but Duple-bodied, T219 is
preserved.

Another London Transport Regal,
an ex-East Surrey bus-bodied
version in the Country fleet, at
Enfield Town.

An oil-engined Regal, with English Electric body, supplied in 1937 to Northern Ireland Transport.

The caption on this 1939 AEC photo reads: 'Linking up villages where there are, in many cases, no longer train services, Everingham Bros AEC Regals not only provide essential transport services, but give country people a standard of travel equal to anything in the big towns.'

The David MacBrayne fleet, serving the Western Highlands of Scotland, contained several AEC Regals of different types. These were two of four 1939 Park Royal-bodied 35-seat coaches, in the distinctive red, cream and green livery.

AEC Regal and Regent, delivered to Salford Corporation in 1936–37 — many fleets standardised on these compatible models. The Regal had a 30-seat rear-entrance English Electric body, and the Regent a 48-seat Metro-Cammell body.

*Above left:* High Street, Huddersfield in wartime, with a 1934 Brush-bodied AEC Regal of Huddersfield Corporation.

*Above:* Aldgate, London, in 1939, and a new Green Line Leyland Tiger underfloor-engined TF coach laying over alongside two AEC Regals of the 10T10 series. The 266 Green Line coaches of this type had bodies built by LPTB at Chiswick.

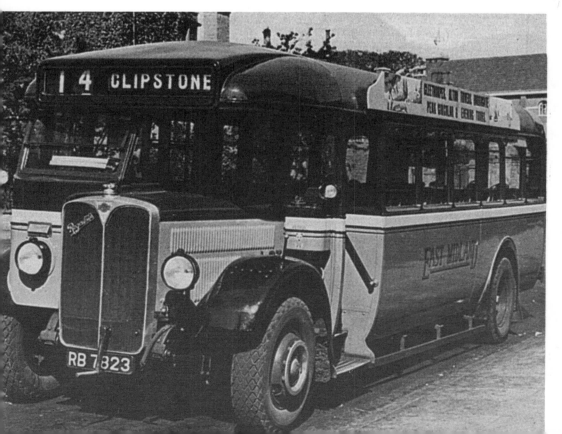

A Regal 4 of East Midland, at Mansfield in 1935. It had a Brush body, with seats for 32.

35

An unusual, though hardly satisfactory, attempt at coach streamlining, on a Duple-bodied Regal 32-seater, supplied to Sutherland, Peterhead, in 1938.

*Right:* A long-lived Daimler COG6 of West Bromwich Corporation; this 1939 Metro-Cammell bodied example was still in service 20 years later.

More successful streamlining, a Harrington dorsal fin body on Regal chassis, supplied to Hawkey's, Newquay, in 1939.

Postwar Burlingham Seagull bodies disguise these Scottish Omnibuses Regals, seen on tour in the Scottish Highlands in the 1950s. The chassis date from 1938–40, and in this form lasted well into the 1960s.

# Daimler CO series

In the earliest days of the motor vehicle the name 'Daimler' could be found on the products of two quite separate concerns. One was Milnes-Daimler, and we have already seen how G. F. Milnes entered an agreement with the Cannstatt Daimler factory in Germany to import commercial vehicle chassis.

Before the Milnes agreement the British engineer Frederick Simms met Gottlieb Daimler in 1890 and acquired all Daimler engine patent rights for Britain. Three years later Simms formed the Daimler Motor Syndicate Ltd, which in 1896 became the Daimler Motor Co Ltd, manufacturing private motor vehicles in Coventry. The German patents ran out in 1901 and Daimler continued to manufacture on its own account. The company's first venture into the motor bus field was the advanced KPL model of 1910, but a patent infingement action over its petrol-electric transmission killed the bus off, and with it Daimler's plans to operate it in service in London.

Enter Frank Searle, whom we met in connection with the London B type bus. Searle joined Daimler in 1911 to develop a commercial vehicle department and he concentrated on producing a conventional bus chassis which had much in common with his B type. This appeared in 1912 and Searle worked hard to obtain sizeable orders for his new 40hp bus, including one for 350, mainly for the Tramways (MET) Omnibus Co, formed by Metropolitan Electric Tramways, at that time independent of London General. At the same time the Underground Electric Railways Group assumed control of London General, and in 1913 General acquired Tramways (MET), along with a part-completed order for 40hp Daimlers and a three-year maintenance contract which had been part of Searle's deal. To release itself from these commitments General offered to appoint Daimler as sole selling agents for any surplus chassis produced by AEC at Walthamstow.

This helped the Daimler company, which had a shortage of space at Coventry, and meant that between 1913 and 1916 Walthamstow-built AECs, fitted with either AEC or Daimler engines, were labelled 'Daimler' — the AEC name was felt to be strongly associated with General.

From 1916 the links were less obvious but not completely dead. In 1926 AEC and Daimler formed the Associated Daimler Co to market the commercial vehicles built by both firms. This time the products carried the ADC name, whether AEC or Daimler designed, whether with AEC or Daimler engines. After two years the two concerns reverted to making and selling commercial vehicle chassis under their own names, although their initial models were, inevitably, similar to latter-day ADC products.

Daimler's postwar excursions into the double-deck field had been fairly limited — the standard chassis of the time which were, in alphabetical progression, the CF6, CG6 and CH6. Each model was an improvement on its predecessor and the CH6 in particular represented a significant advance.

The feature which distinguished the CH6 and marked an important turning-point in the Daimler story was the Wilson preselective epicyclic gearbox coupled to a fluid flywheel. This allowed drivers to select gear at a suitable time, and effect the change with a pedal which replaced the normal clutch pedal. The gearbox was immediately adopted for Daimler cars and commercials, and was to remain standard on Daimler buses for many years.

The next Daimler bus chassis to appear was the CP6, which was the CH6 with a 6.56 litre poppet valve engine in place of the 5.76 litre sleeve valve unit previously fitted.

But there were other important technological developments in the air. The diesel engine had obvious applications for bus work, and many manufacturers and operators were engaged in experimental work. The appearance of the legendary Gardner LW oil engines in 1931 really started the spread of the diesel, and in the year ending September 1935 around one-third of new buses registered in Britain were diesel-engined.

Some chassis manufacturers concentrated on developing their own diesel engines, but others plumped for the Gardner product, which had already earned itself a good name for performance and reliability. Daimler's first oil-engined chassis was the COG5 of 1933, in many ways a CP6 with the 7 litre 5LW (five-cylinder) Gardner engine. The combination of Gardner diesel and preselective gearbox had an obvious appeal for bus operators, particularly those with busy urban work, and the COG5, in single-deck and double-deck form, was an instant success.

For Coventry Corporation the COA6 model was developed, with the six-cylinder AEC 7.7 litre engine, and this was built between 1934 and 1940. For other operators requiring the extra power of a six-cylinder engine the COG6 was added to the range in 1936, fitted with the 8.4 litre Gardner 6LW engine.

The CO chassis really established Daimler in the front-line of Britain's bus manufacturers, for the range filled an important gap in the model lists by providing a bus with the power and ease of handling ideal for even the most arduous city work.

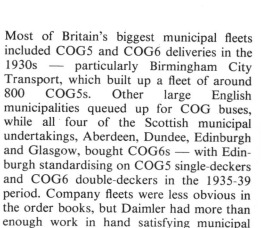

The chassis layout of the Daimler COG5 appears very simple by present-day standards.

Most of Britain's biggest municipal fleets included COG5 and COG6 deliveries in the 1930s — particularly Birmingham City Transport, which built up a fleet of around 800 COG5s. Other large English municipalities queued up for COG buses, while all four of the Scottish municipal undertakings, Aberdeen, Dundee, Edinburgh and Glasgow, bought COG6s — with Edinburgh standardising on COG5 single-deckers and COG6 double-deckers in the 1935-39 period. Company fleets were less obvious in the order books, but Daimler had more than enough work in hand satisfying municipal fleets.

The preselective gearbox had obvious attractions for London work, but London Transport did not buy COG5s or COG6s. London General had bought three Daimler CH6s in 1930 to test the transmission, and after fitting Daimler gearboxes to AEC Renowns, started to specify preselective boxes in many new deliveries. The Daimler box was also available to other AEC customers until 1934 when AEC introduced its own version. While other chassis of the 1930s were often available with a choice of gearboxes and even engines, the COG5/COG6 range was remarkably standardised, offering the minimum of choice. The first significant addition to the range was the COG5/40 model of 1936, which catered for those operators looking for maximum capacity in single-deckers within the 27ft 6in (8.38m) overall length. This was achieved with an upright radiator and a more compact engine compartment and driver's cab. Over 400 COG5/40s were built. A double-deck equivalent was the COG5/60, developed for Coventry Corporation in 1939/40; the suffix in the model designations for both the single-deck and double-deck models referred to the potential seating capacity.

By 1940 when heavy air raids on Coventry forced production to a halt around 1,900 CO double-deckers and 400 single-deckers had been built. Production was transferred to Wolverhampton in 1942, and in 1943 100 wartime double-deck chassis were built. Designated CWG5 they were basically COG5 but with cast iron in place of valuable light alloys. The CWG5 was succeeded by the CWA6 later in 1943, which used the AEC 7.7 litre engine, and more than 800 of these were built.

Daimler had been developing its own diesel engine for some time, and this eventually appeared in 1945 as the 8.6 litre CD6 unit. Between 1945 and 1947 many of Daimler's last 'wartime' chassis had this engine, and were designated CWD6. In all some 1,400 CW chassis were built in four years.

The return to peace brought the CV range in 1946/47 — initially with Daimler's CD6 engine (CVD6) and then with the 5LW and 6LW Gardners (CVG5/CVG6). The chassis owed much to the CO range, and survived in production until 1968 — a tribute to the inherent soundness of a bus designed 35 years earlier.

Many CO range buses put in more than 20 years good service, and some passed the 25 year mark. Four are preserved today — the

This early COG6 was built in 1935 as a demonstrator, with Weymann 54-seat body, and in 1936 was bought by Aberdeen Corporation. It operated on loan to London Transport in 1940/41, and returned north to give good service in Aberdeen until 1958.

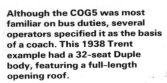
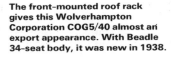

best known is a survivor of the big Birmingham City Transport fleet of COG5s. Built in 1937, CVP 207 had the traditional Birmingham style of body, in this case built by Metro-Cammell. It remained in the Birmingham fleet until 1961, when it was sold to a dealer; in 1964 it was rescued for preservation. Alan Townsin rode back from the 1965 HCVC Brighton Run on CVP 207, and wrote in *Buses Illustrated*:

'To be frank, I was never a great enthusiast for the COG5, much preferring the 6LW-powered COG6, because of its increased smoothness at least as much as its extra power. I must, therefore, confess that I was surprised how quiet and vibration-free 1107 was, inside. The BCT style of trim, with moquette-covered front bulkhead, probably helped. Daimler, however, was undoubtedly the first maker to evolve a really satisfactory flexible engine mounting, and virtually none of the vibration that emanantes from the 5 cylinder Gardner engine reached the passengers. It so happened that I rode in a 6LX-powered Fleetline the following day and

there was little to choose between it and the COG5 for vibration.

'Another factor in the noise problem may well have been Daimler's continued use of the floating cab structure in COG5 days. This was an old-fashioned idea with numerous draught-sealing and rattle problems and had been abandoned by most other makers years earlier. The cab floor, front dash and bonnet assembly were all mounted on the chassis instead of being built into the body. Noise is likely to be magnified by sheet metal parts, but the Daimler system seems likely to have had the virtue of not transmitting it to the interior of the bus.

'The most prominent sound was the far-from-unpleasant note of the preselection gearbox. Someone said that BCT driving instructors taught their pupils that this type of gearbox ought to 'sing' during gear changes. Certainly some very smooth changes were obtained by Barry Ware and, later, Peter Hardy, during the run, accompanied by an effect not unlike a contralto running up and down her scales.'

*Above:* Edinburgh Corporation standardised on COG5 single-deckers and COG6 double-deckers between 1935-39. This COG6 with Metro-Cammell body, new in 1938, is tilt-tested at Edinburgh's Shrubhill Works.

*Far left:* Preserved Birmingham COG5/Metro-Cammell 1107 in the appropriate surroundings of the Bull Ring on a rally in 1972.

*Left:* Coventry Corporation favoured the AEC-engined COA6 model, and this Brush-bodied example is seen in Hales Street, Coventry when new in 1937.

41

South Africa was a lucrative Daimler market, and several fleets took delivery of COG6 models. These 1939 deliveries for Durban Corporation had Metro-Cammell bodies of typically British appearance — except that they were 8ft wide, when 7ft 6in was the British maximum.

The war meant that five COG6/Metro-Cammell built for Johannesburg Transport in 1941 could not be exported, and, although 8ft wide, they were diverted to British operators. Four went to Birmingham Corporation, and the fifth, seen here, to West Mon Board, in Wales.

*Right:* London Transport RT2586, on tram-replacement route 70 in south London in 1951, shows well the classic, timeless lines of the RT design.

Several COG5s were rebodied for further service after the war, including this 1938 Trent example, rebodied by Willowbrook in 1946, seen in 1952 in Derby.

# AEC Regent RT

One of the most significant buses in the development of the modern double-decker started life rather ignominiously, disguised by an elderly second-hand body, and carrying a misleading fleet number. Underneath an open-staircase body from a Leyland Titan was a brand-new chassis — the prototype of what was to become the biggest class of buses ever operated by London Transport.

London had largely stuck with AEC for its double-deck requirements in the 1930s. At first the Regent and six-wheel Renown were bought, and from 1933 the longer-wheelbase Regent was favoured, forming the STL class which grew to over 2,600 buses in the years 1933-42. The STL Regents, latterly with 7.7 litre diesel engines and preselective gearboxes, were successful vehicles, and London Transport was working on its successor for the 1940s. An important ingredient was to be a bigger engine, suitably derated, and an air-operated preselective gearbox and air-pressure brakes. The prototype chassis appeared in 1938, registered EYK 396, and ran for a while with an old TD class body as ST1140.

In April 1939 a new body was built, a 26ft (7.92m) long by 7ft 6in (2.28m) wide four-bay body, with classically smooth and timeless lines. A feature of the new bus, now reclassified RT1, was a sloping bonnet, which gave the driver excellent forward and side vision. A further 150 RTs appeared between November 1939 and June 1940, but the war brought to an end production of what was in effect a very advanced and luxurious peacetime vehicle. One other RT chassis was built at this time, and fitted with a Weymann body for Glasgow Corporation. It seems likely that this was destined for the 1939 Commercial Motor Show, which was never held, and it is possible that the RT would have gone into volume production for 1940 if war had not intervened.

The AEC Regent had first appeared in 1929, with a 6.1 litre petrol engine, and its development in the 1930s paralleled that of its single-deck stablemate, the Regal. A bigger, 7.4 litre, petrol engine replaced the original unit in 1931, but from 1930 oil engines were fitted to AEC Regents. Daimler preselective gearboxes were available from 1932, with AEC's own unit succeeding it in 1934. The famous 7.7 litre oil engine was introduced in 1934, although some operators still opted for petrol engines, and others preferred the beefier 8.8 litre oiler. The engine fitted to the 152 'prewar' RTs was bigger still, a 9.6 litre unit developing 115bhp.

After World War II AEC's immediate answer to the urgent need for double-deckers was the Regent Mk II, equivalent to the normal prewar Regent, with 7.7 litre engine and four-speed crash box. Around 700 were sold between 1945 and 1947. In 1946 the Regent Mk III appeared, and this was very much the 1938 RT chassis reborn. It was available generally and around 70 chassis were built between late 1946 and mid 1947. But not for London; these first Regent IIIs were snapped up by operators throughout Britain, although the bodies fitted rarely matched the sleek good looks of the prewar London Transport-built body.

London's first new postwar deliveries were bought for quick delivery, and included Daimler CWA6s and Leyland Titan PD1s, as well as 20 AEC Regent IIs which were added to the STL class. Production of London's own RTs started in earnest in mid 1947 and continued until 1953. In that period 4,674 RT chassis were built, and fitted with standard bodies, mainly by Park Royal and Weymann, but also by Saunders, and non-standard bodies by Cravens.

The standard body was largely to the 1939 design, but had detail differences, the most notable being a straight bottom edge to the driver's windscreen instead of the curved edge on the 'prewar' buses.

The RT had now become very much a London model, apart from 40 London-type Park Royal-bodied RTs for St Helens

The one extra 'prewar' RT chassis was built by AEC for Glasgow Corporation, and received a Weymann 56-seat body which was attractive in itself, but which lacked the symmetry of the London-designed RT body.

The Glasgow RT could have been the first of many production chassis built from 1940, had not the war intervened.

RT1 reborn. The original 1939 LPTB body of RT1, fitted to a newer chassis reappeared in original form in 1979. It is seen here at Battersea in the Easter Parade that year — a worthy addition to the preserved ranks.

The first postwar RT chassis were not for London Transport, and appeared in fleets throughout Britain. This 1947 Devon General example, at Exmouth in 1955, had a Weymann body.

Another provincial RT, a Douglas Corporation example of 1947 had a Northern Counties body.

Corporation in 1950/52. 'Provincial' orders were satisfied with the Regent Mk III series 2, which was largely based on the RT, complete with 9.6 litre engine and preselective gearbox, but with a higher-set radiator to accommodate the air-cleaner. While London received its RTs at a rate of around 600 a year, other customers bought the Regent III in large numbers — some with later options like the 7.7 litre engine and crash gearbox. London Transport also bought 'provincial' Regent IIIs, however — 76 lowbridge 53-seaters bought in 1950/52 with standard Weymann bodies, the RLH class.

Delivery of the London RTs allowed a speedy replacement of the remaining prewar buses and the non-standard wartime and early postwar vehicles. It also allowed London Transport to complete its tram replacement in 1952. After the boom of the early postwar years, though, the demand for public transport started to drop in the mid-1950s, and London found itself with too many buses. This led to several new RTs being placed in store and in fact some did not enter service until after the first appearance of the RT's replacement.

The RT was not only built in AEC form. Leyland PD2 Titans were supplied from 1948 to 1954 to a London specification, as the RTL and RTW classes. The 1,631 RTLs were 7ft 6in (2.28m) wide, as the RTs, while the 500 RTWs were built to the new legal maximum width of 8ft (2.43m).

There were other RT variants. There were the 160 SRTs, a marriage of new RT bodies and late pre-war STL chassis, to cope with delays in delivery of new RT chassis. This happened in 1949, and although there were to have been 300 more SRTs, the situation improved and no more were built. The SRT bodies were mounted on new RT chassis in 1954.

An RT with an unusual history was RT97, badly damaged in 1944, and rebuilt in 1945 as a pay-as-you-board vehicle with platform door and seated conductor. It lasted only a short time in this guise before reappearing in 1949 as RTC1, heavily rebuilt as a most attractive double-deck coach: but even in this form it was short-lived in LT service.

The fast and manoeuvrable RT was to be found everywhere in the London system, for by 1954, adding in the RTL and RTW Leylands, there were almost 7,000 members of the family in stock. In addition to the familiar red RT in service in central London, there were red RTs in London's suburbs, and green RTs in LT's Country Area, and in the Green Line fleet.

New RTs lined up in 1950, ready for tram replacement duties, showing the close attention to detail and the classic gently sloping front end profile.

*Right:* A former London Transport RT in the service of Cape Tramways, in South Africa. The famous Table Mountain, with its 'table–cloth' cloud cover, is seen in the background.

RT withdrawals started as early as 1955 when the prewar vehicles were taken from passenger service, and in 1956 the non-standard Cravens-bodied buses were sold and were eagerly snapped up for further service. Other RTs soon followed, and could soon be found in service in Britain and overseas, many with independent fleets, but also in municipal service, for examples were bought by Bradford and Dundee Corporations.

Withdrawal of the RT family was inevitably a slow process. The two Leyland variants went fairly early, but the standard AEC product was to linger on for more than two decades, with a regular and steady trickle of sales. The high degree of standardisation helped to ensure a long and successful lifespan, for the RTs were the largest batch of buses to a standard specification ever supplied to one operator — and that feat is unlikely to be matched in the future. London's excellent maintenance system also ensured that the high standards were kept, and meant that virtually a new bus emerged after each overhaul.

From the start the postwar RT had been designed with mass-production in mind, so parts were built to identical drawings by Park Royal and Weymann and assembled on identical jigs — useful experience gained from London Transport's wartime experience in aircraft production. When standard RTs were overhauled, the chassis and body were separated for individual attention, never to be reunited. For this reason RTs with very low bonnet numbers, implying 1947 deliveries, survived into 1979 in London service, suggesting 32 years' service. In a normal fleet this would be the case, but it was difficult to know how much of the

**PARK ROYAL**
56-SEATER DOUBLE DECK METAL BODY ON A.E.C. CHASSIS. IN CONSTANT SERVICE IN THE CAPITAL AND CHOSEN FOR THE AMERICAN & CANADIAN TOUR.

**PARK ROYAL VEHICLES LTD.**
ABBEY ROAD, PARK ROYAL, LONDON, N.W. IO. ELGAR 6522

Two London RTs, and a Leyland RTL, were sent to the United States and Canada in 1952 for a 12,000-mile goodwill tour, and Park Royal did not miss the opportunity to mention the fact in contemporary advertising.

Back from North America, RT2776, RTL1307 and RT2775 at Earls Court in October 1952.

London RT — apart, perhaps from the registration plate — had been around since 1947. Nonetheless, in these days of a 12-15-year maximum vehicle life, the survival of the RT over a 30-year lifespan is a remarkable achievement — all the more remarkable when it is recalled that the basic design dated back to 1938, and the final RT withdrawals from London service occurred almost exactly 40 years after RT1 entered service.

After many years when there were literally nothing but RTs to be seen on many London streets, in the late 1970s it became an increasing problem to find them, concentrated as they were in several isolated pockets. The London Transport RT fleet had been depleted in 1970 when the Country Area operations passed to National Bus Company as London Country Bus Services Ltd. Included in the transfer were 484 RTs, but although London Country was anxious to update its inherited fleet, the RTs were required to linger on for several years, some running latterly in NBC's corporate leaf green livery. The story did not end there, however, as 34 London Country RTs returned to London Transport to help ease a vehicle shortage.

The 'provincial' Regent Mk III was succeeded by the Regent Mk V in 1954, and this remained in production until 1968. With around 8,000 Regent Mk IIIs and 2,600 Regent Mk Vs added to the 7,000 prewar and 700 Regent Mk II, the Regent production from 1929 to 1968 totalled over 18,000 vehicles. London sales accounted for roughly 46% of this total.

Inevitably in a bus that was universally popular, with operators, engineers, passengers and enthusiasts, there are many Regents preserved for posterity. These include 33 prewar buses, over 80 of the Regent Mk II/III/V families — *plus* a veritable fleet of RTs. There are six 'prewar' RTs preserved, plus over 60 postwar examples; this should perhaps be qualified with the phrase 'at the time of writing', for the withdrawal of the RT from passenger service in London, in a blaze of glory in April 1979, opened up further opportunities for preservationists to acquire roadworthy specimens. And there was the slightly ironic situation where London Transport was hiring preserved RTs to assist with its driver training programme.

But the RT did not disappear completely from London's streets, and perhaps it never will. One thing is certain — with so many preserved RTs throughout the country, and indeed the world, it will remain a familiar sight for many years to come.

RTs were eagerly snapped up by other operators when London Transport started withdrawals, and many came to operators in Scotland. This was an early sale, to the Ayrshire co-operative A1 Service group.

Birmingham City Transport received 15 of these RT-type Regents in 1947, with Park Royal 54-seat bodies. No 1634, seen when new, demonstrates the rather uneasy match of contemporary London and Birmingham ideas.

49

*Above left:* The 120 Craven-bodied RTs for London Transport had five-bay bodies based on the bodybuilder's standard product. The former RT1456 is seen in Mansfield in 1956, in the service of Wass Bros, the independent taken over by East Midland the following year.

*Above:* The 40 St Helens Corporation RTs had Park Royal bodies to London specification. The use made of the LT front destination display is unusual.

*Right:* Uncompromisingly utility in its specification — one of the fleet of Massey-bodied Guy Arabs delivered in 1943-45 to Stockport Corporation.

*Left:* RT3333 seen in pleasant surroundings in Swanley in 1969 in the green of London Transport's Country Area.

*Below:* Eight London RTs lined up at Birds Commercial Motors, Stratford-on-Avon, the dealer which bought and re-sold many RTs in the 1950s and 1960s. This photograph was taken in 1964.

# Guy Arab utility

HEATON MERSEY

JA 7613

The outbreak of war in September 1939 did not bring bus production grinding to a halt. Many outstanding orders, particularly for double-deckers and single-deck service buses, were supplied to the high standards of comfort and finish that had been achieved by 1939. The 'prewar' batch of London AEC RTs was just one example, and for over a year chassis and body manufacturers struggled to complete the orders they had in hand. As the war situation deteriorated, new bus building was stopped in 1941, and all stocks of spare parts and partly-built buses were 'frozen' on Government instructions. This allowed an opportunity to assess the seriousness of the situation, and to satisfy the urgent requirements of many of the operators most affected by the hostilities, the regulations were relaxed and the parts and buses were 'unfrozen'.

The resulting mixture of around 450 buses was allocated to the operators with the most pressing needs — rarely the operator which had ordered them. Some were very much peacetime buses; others were built to a much more basic specification, devoid of curved panels and other 'frills'. This was an acceptable short-term measure, but as the war dragged on, a longer view had to be taken. The result was the birth of the utility bus.

There was just one single-deck model, the 32-seat normal control Bedford OWB, but double-deck building was entrusted to several chassis and body builders. At first Guy and Leyland were each asked to supply 500 double-deck chassis, but the facilities at Leyland were switched to the production of tanks, tank engines, bombs and shells. In 1943 Daimler managed to bounce back with its wartime version of the COG5 chassis, and Bristol returned to the bus scene with its utility K models in 1944/45. But it was largely left to Guy to supply the bulk of Britain's wartime buses — around 2,500 of the total of around 4,000 utility double-deckers.

Guy's involvement in utility buses is an interesting story. Sydney S. Guy left the Sunbeam Motor Co to form Guy Motors Ltd in 1914. His move was a successful one, and the rugged Guy chassis found a ready market for use in lorries and buses. In the difficult years after World War I Guy tried car production, but quickly returned to the commercial vehicle market. His bus models were often small-capacity chassis, but in 1924 Guy produced an early drop-frame model, and went on to more ambitious things with a normal control six-wheel double-decker in 1926. The Guy name was closely associated with six-wheelers until 1933 when the new Arab chassis was introduced, the first production bus chassis range to offer an

52

oil engine as standard. The engines chosen were the Gardner LW series, first introduced in 1931, and Guy offered the 4LW and 5LW in single-deck Arabs, and the 5LW and 6LW in double-deck Arabs.

The engine choice was a sound one, and Arabs found favour with a restricted circle of buyers. By 1935, however, most of Guy's production was concentrated on War Department trucks, and few Arabs were built — though Burton Corporation did take a batch in 1940.

With the outbreak of war Guy was lined up to produce searchlight vehicles, but this order was cancelled, and the double-deck order was placed in 1941. The specification for Guy's wartime double-decker was finalised in September 1941, and the first prototype was ready in less than six months. It materialised as the Arab Mk I, outwardly different from its 1933 namesake, but mechanically similar. The Gardner 5LW engine was there, with crash gearbox, although the new chassis was much heavier, due to the use of cast iron in place of valuable lighter alloys.

The first 500 Arabs were quickly built, and bodybuilders rushed them to operators all over Britain. Most had the 7 litre 5LW engine, but a few operators with hilly or awkward terrain were allowed the 8.4 litre 6LW. An AEC 7.7 litre engine had been loaned for experimental installation, but the AEC engines were fitted in Bristol and Daimler utilities, while Guys stuck to the Gardners.

For operators and passengers alike the Arab was a godsend, in spite of the utility specification. Drivers used to preselective gearboxes had to re-learn old skills on the notorious Guy gearbox; passengers had to endure the rigours of wooden-slatted seats. But they were valuable people-movers, and were distributed where most required by the Ministry of War Transport.

Hot on the heels of the first 500 Arabs came the Arab Mk II, which featured a longer chassis — 26ft 5in (8.05m) — to accommodate a longer bonnet for the alternative 6LW engine. All Mk IIs, whether 5LW or 6LW engines, were built with this feature to simplify production, although the 5LW unit was by far the more familiar. Between 1943 and 1946 some 2,000 Arab Mk IIs were built, and were allocated to fleets of all sizes in all parts of Britain. Independent, municipal and company fleets all had utility Arabs, and the largest fleet was built up between 1942 and 1945 by London Transport with a fleet of 435 buses.

A lowbridge Roe-bodied Arab II delivered to the Leicestershire independent Kemp & Shaw in 1943.

By comparison with the drab brown of the Kemp & Shaw bus, this Maidstone Corporation Arab I, with Duple 56-seat body, was delivered in this amazingly ornate peacetime livery early in 1943.

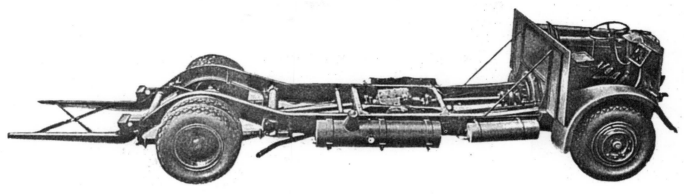

The sturdy Arab utility double-deck chassis.

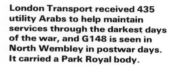

London Transport received 435 utility Arabs to help maintain services through the darkest days of the war, and G148 is seen in North Wembley in postwar days. It carried a Park Royal body.

Bristol Tramways added a small number of Arabs to its fleet, and this 1943 example had a Park Royal body.

Scottish Omnibuses bought nine former London Transport Arabs in 1951/52. Like the others, E28, seen here in 1952, was operated for a short time before being rebuilt and rebodied as a single-decker. New in 1946, it had a Park Royal body.

One of the resulting rebuilt London Arabs, which reappeared in 1954 with new 30ft long Scottish Omnibuses 39-seat bodies, suitably re-registered. Four similar buses went to Highland Omnibuses.

Guy's wartime effort was a remarkable achievement. The company suddenly found itself Britain's major bus chassis builder, where previously buses had only been a small part of the output from Wolverhampton. From March 1942, when the first utility Arab prototype was complete it took little more than 18 months to build the first 1,000 chassis. By December 1944 another 1,000 had been supplied, helped by the advanced moving track installed in 1942 for chassis assembly.

Production of the Arab Mk II trickled on until 1946, with later examples carrying bodies which indicated a gradual and welcome return to peacetime standards. That same year the Arab Mk III was introduced, with a constant mesh gearbox, and a lower radiator and bonnet level; the Arab Mk III sold well until 1952, some examples with Meadows engines, preselective gearboxes or air brakes. The Arab Mk IV appeared in 1950, largely to a Birmingham City Transport specification; its most obvious difference was the 'new look' tin front which concealed the Guy radiator, although some exposed radiator chassis were built. The squarer 'Johannesburg' front was fitted to some Arab Mk IVs, while some chassis had semi-automatic gearboxes.

During the Arab Mk IV model's life a second, and very different, Guy double-deck model was introduced. This was the amazing Wulfrunian, with a front-mounted Gardner 6LX engine *and* a set-back front axle to permit an entrance at the extreme front; other unusual features included air suspension and disc brakes. The Arab Mk IV was itself succeeded by the Arab Mk V, which stuck to a conventional layout, but with a lower frame. This guaranteed it a longer and more successful life than the poor Wulfrunian, which was only offered from 1959 to 1965; the Arab Mk V was available

Alexanders (Fife) inherited 73 utility Arabs when the Alexander company was split up in 1961, and some survived until 1968. These three examples with Northern Counties bodies are seen in Glasgow in 1964.

Many Scottish Omnibuses utility Arabs were transferred for further service to Highland Omnibuses. This 1945 6LW-engined Arab with Weymann lowbridge bodywork is seen at the Dounreay Nuclear Reactor in 1966.

Edinburgh Corporation bought 60 ex-London Arabs in 1952/53, rebuilt the chassis and rebodied them with 8ft wide Duple/Nudd 55-seat bodies. This bus started life as London G419, and survived in the form shown until 1969.

Another rebodied utility Arab — this East Midland example, seen at Mansfield garage in 1954, was new in 1945 with a Roe body, and in 1954 received this new Roe lowbridge body.

from 1962 until 1970/71, and for part of its life it was joined by a very Guy-like model from Daimler — by then, like Guy, part of the Jaguar group. This was the Daimler CCG5/CCG6, basically the well-proved CV chassis with Guy constant mesh gearbox.

The Arab family had been on the British market for nearly 40 years, and in the middle part of this period, in the 1940s and 1950s, it was a popular choice with many operators, and become a familiar sight, particularly on busy urban work for which it was well suited.

But the utility models are probably the most fondly remembered. They enjoyed a long life, and many saw 20 years' service. The sturdy chassis had plenty of life in them, although the bodies, often built using unsatisfactory material, were less happy. Many operators rebuilt extensively their utility bodies in the postwar years, while others had new bodies built on utility chassis.

The sizeable London Arab fleet was sold in the early 1950s, and eagerly snapped up by operators throughout Britain and abroad. Perhaps the most interesting use was made of the London Guys by Edinburgh Corporation, which in 1952 bought 60 of them. The bodies were removed, the chassis reconditioned, and new 8ft (2.43m) wide Duple/Nudd bodies were mounted on them. The Guy radiator was hidden behind an ornate full-width grille, and as front-line tram-replacement buses, and latterly as rush-hour extras, the buses stayed in Edinburgh service until 1969 — a good deal longer than the 8-10 years in London.

One of the Edinburgh ex-London Guys is now preserved, one of 18 Mk I and Mk II Arabs which are still with us, serving as a reminder of the buses that kept Britain moving throughout the war — and for many years afterwards.

*Right:* The familiar front end of the Bedford OB with Duple Vista body. This 1950 example was delivered to Starks, Dunbar, and passed with that fleet to Scottish Omnibuses in 1964. It is now preserved.

# Bedford OB

Most of the British bus manufacturers have concentrated on catering for the requirements of the majority of operators: and the majority have tended to look for bigger and bigger buses, with more and more seats. As legislation has been relaxed over the years, so the buses have steadily grown; from the 22ft 6.5in (6.87m) of the 1910 London B type we have come to the age of the 39ft 4in (12m) bus — and even articulated buses up to 59ft (18m). The B type had seats for 34 passengers, while modern double-deckers can carry up to 86, and it seems that where urban operations are concerned, capacity is the answer.

Yet at the same time there have been a sizeable number of smaller operators who have looked for smaller buses, often because of physical restrictions; but sometimes because they recognised their limitations, and rarely had a need for seating more than 20 or 30 passengers.

The interest in small-capacity buses grew in the years after World War I. Full-size bus chassis of the time were high-built and cumbersome on solid tyres. The appearance of nippy pneumatic-tyred small bus chassis, often imported from Europe and the United States, was the signal for a boom in the growth of the bus business. Men who had gained mechanical experience in the war used their gratuities to purchase the little Chevrolets, Fiats, GMCs, Internationals, Lancias and Reos that flooded on to the British market. And often they used them where they wished, for there was no national system of route licensing; the new breed of busmen ran their buses on new services, on existing bus services, on tram routes. They fought the established operators, and each other, for the best pickings. The result on the roads was often chaotic, with unrestricted competition; the result for the manufacturers was a bonanza, at first for the imported vehicles and then, as British builders caught up, for home models like the Albions, Dennises, Commers and Thornycrofts.

The improved British-made small chassis stemmed the flow of imported buses, but it did not really stop until the appearance of a new model made in Britain — but by an American-owned firm. The chassis was the Bedford, built by Vauxhall, owned by General Motors.

Vauxhall started building cars in 1903, and two years later moved to Luton. In 1925 the Vauxhall company passed into the control of the American giant General Motors. During the 1920s GM-built Chevrolet chassis were imported into Britain for lighter-weight bus and truck work, and from 1929 Chevrolet cars and commercials had been produced at Luton. The next logical step was a more definitely 'British' model, and in April 1931 there emerged from Luton a new 2-ton truck, similar to the Chevrolet, but carrying the name Bedford, after the county of its birth. This was appropriate, for a great deal of Luton thinking had gone into the new model.

The immediate success of the new Bedford 2-tonners was repeated when bus models followed in August 1931, the 14-seat WHB and 20-seat WLB. The chassis were competitively priced, at £250 for the WHB and £265 for the WLB.

The Bedford bus made an immediate impact on the market; the new chassis were mopping up more than half the market in the first three months in production, and this steadily increased; the 20-seat WLB was by far the more popular bus model, and the smaller WHB was dropped after less than two years. The WLB continued on the model lists until late in 1935, but some operators were specifying an adaptation of a new goods model, the WTL, for their buses and coaches.

The WT range of 3-ton trucks first appeared late in 1933, and went into production a few months later. They caused a minor sensation, for they introduced the semi-forward control layout, where the driver sat behind the front axle, but alongside part of the engine. Externally the bonnet was much shorter, as the engine was over the front axle, and the result was a gain in space, better load distribution and a neater appearance. Late in 1935 the proper bus version of the WT range, the WTB, was introduced, and in its four-year life more than 3,000 chassis were built. The truck models were equally successful, and Bedford could justifiably use the advertising slogan 'You see them everywhere'.

Late in 1937 it received a new 28hp Bedford petrol engine, and a new style of rounded radiator grille, with horizontal slats — probably the most instantly recognisable Bedford grille of all time.

Successor to the WTB was the OB, introduced in August 1939 — hardly the ideal time to introduce a new model, as it turned out. The OB had the 28hp petrol engine and a 14ft 6in (4.41m) wheelbase, which normally allowed seats up to 26, again with the semi-forward control layout of the WTB. Only 73 OBs — 52 home and 21 export — were built until the war forced production to cease in October 1939. But the OB was due for an early revival, and a distinguished career.

With the war situation deteriorating, the cessation of bus production and the eventual relaxation which allowed release of the 'unfrozen' vehicles, many operators were desperate for new buses. We have seen how

Guy, and to a lesser degree Daimler and Bristol, supplied Britain's double-deck needs in the war years, and although capacity was the first consideration for many, there were operators of all sizes with a pressing need for a new single-deck bus. Only one model was offered, the Bedford OWB, which was essentially the OB of 1939. A 32-seat utility body was designed, and built mainly by Duple, but also by Roe, Mulliner and SMT.

The OWB chassis retained the 1938 grille and looked neat married to the utility body, which was well-proportioned and practical. At just £810 complete it was a useful buy and that more than 3,300 OWBs were built in just over three and a half years is all the more remarkable when it is recalled that Bedford was a major supplier of military trucks, roughly 1,000 a week throughout the war.

After hostilities production switched back to the OB in October 1945, and it soon became a familiar sight on the roads of Britain and abroad. The most famous version carried a 29-seat coach body first introduced in 1939 — the Duple Vista. With its gently curved waistline, slim window pillars and well-proportioned lines, the Vista was an all-time classic, and continued a tradition of close links between Bedford and Duple. The traffic boom of the early postwar years and the apparently insatiable demand for new buses and coaches spawned a host of small bodybuilding firms in literally every corner of Britain. Many built on the OB, and some tried to imitate the Vista body, but none succeeded in catching the well-considered subtlety of the Duple design.

The reliability of the OWB had attracted many new customers to Bedford, and company and even municipal fleets ordered OBs, mainly for coach touring work. Many OWBs at the same time were enjoying a fresh lease of life with new bodies — often the Duple Vista.

The mechanical specification of the OB still owed something to the original WHB and WLB of 1931, for Bedford had sensibly chosen to improve the design gradually over the years, rather than make dramatic changes. So the OB had the 72bhp 28hp petrol engine and four-speed gearbox, and the formula was a successful one; the only significant departure from the standard specification was the fitment of the Perkins P6 diesel engine by some operators. The OB chassis was offered with a beefier 'Extra Duty' engine in March 1950 — still a 28hp unit, but developing 84bhp.

In little more than five years 12,693 OBs

were built, of which 43 per cent were for customers overseas — these were the years when the all-out export drive was essential to rebuild the British economy. It was surprising, therefore, that the OB was dropped just a month after the introduction of the new S type 'Big Bedfords' in October 1950. The S type range were full forward-control chassis, with the new 4.9 litre 300 petrol engine; the passenger model was the SB, which could accommodate 33-seat bodies. Clearly Bedford felt that size and increased capacity were wanted — and of course that suited many operators. But there must have been as many operators again for whom the OB was ideal, and in retrospect it seems odd that the model was discontinued as its sales peak.

The SB was not to suffer such a fate. It got bigger and was offered with diesel engines, but stayed on the model lists even after the appearance of its replacement, the VAM, in 1965, and the VAM's replacement, the YRQ, in 1970. It has even survived the introduction of the YRQ's replacement, the YLQ, and even though sales are limited, the SB still caters for a particular segment of the market.

For the operators requiring a 29-seater, the disappearance of the OB left a large gap in the market. Other manufacturers tried to fill the gap, without much success. There were even conversions of current smaller Bedford goods models, but again without notable success. The happiest solution came in 1961 with the VAS, essentially a shorter SB which is coach form could accommodate 29 passengers — often with the appropriately-named Duple Bella Vista body. But the VAS never attained the success of the faithful OB. Small buses, now dubbed midis, made a brief comeback in the 1970s, and Bedford broke new ground with a highly competent rear-engined midibus, the JJL, offered as a complete vehicle.

But the JJL is sophisticated where the OB was simple, and will have little appeal for the country independent or the small coach firm, for whom the OB was the ideal vehicle. Without a suitable replacement, the only answer was — the OB. They soldiered on with their existing OBs, and bought second-hand examples; they cannibalised others to keep them on the road. There are still OBs in service in Britain as I write this — which places them between 30 and 35 years old. They are popular with preservationists, with more than 100 in safe keeping — the vast majority with Duple coach bodies. There are few rallies held in Britain which do not feature at least one OB, and the characteristic gearbox whine which was once a familiar sound all over the country.

The classic lines of the Duple Vista body are shown to good advantage in this official view of a 1948 OB delivered to Kendricks, Dudley.

*Left:* Several operators rebodied utility Bedford OWBs with Duple Vista bodies, and in this form they were indistinguishable from new OBs. This Edinburgh Corporation OWB was new in 1942, and was rebodied in 1949.

One of the many preserved OBs — this 1950 example was new to Harris, Stourport, and is seen on the 1977 Bristol Bus Rally.

The straight-waisted Duple bus body on OB chassis was a less familiar sight. This example was new to the Metropolitan Police, but latterly operated with Eltys Motors of Maenclochog, in Dyfed. It is seen on a school contract in 1974.

Mulliner also produced a bus body for the OB, and this Isle of Man Road Services example is seen pulling out of West Baldwin in 1967, during its last week in service.

This OB with rare Associated Coach Builders 29-seat body was operated on stage service for Steeples, Parwich, in 1956.

*Right:* The familiar shape of the Bristol Lodekka in its long forward entrance FLF6G form. This 1966 example is seen in Nottingham in Midland General service.

**Bristol Lodekka**

Milestones in double-deck bus design seem to be placed at roughly 11-year intervals. The Leyland TD1 (1927) and AEC RT (1938) each contributed greatly to the development of the buses that followed, and, appropriately, in 1949 there appeared a design which took the low-height double-decker one important stage further.

This was the prototype Bristol/Eastern Coach Works Lodekka, the first bus which successfully achieved a low overall height (13ft 4in; 4.06m) with normal seating on both decks. Britain's Victorian legacy of low railway bridges meant that many operators required lowbridge buses on busy services. This was most noticeable among independent or company fleets with inter-urban services, but there were also municipal operators which required some or all double-deckers to be no more than around 13ft 6in (4.11m) high.

The most common solution was the lowbridge side-gangway arrangement, popularised by the Leyland Titan TD1. The low upper deck offside gangway created a slight inconvenience on the lower deck, while the four-across bench seating upstairs achieved maximum capacity without too many problems for passengers, particularly on longer journeys. It would be misleading to describe the lowbridge arrangement as 'popular', but in the absence of anything better it was tolerated if maximum seating capacity was required. Today's big single-deckers, offering space (if not a seat) for as many passengers as a double-decker, were not possible with the 27ft 6in (8.38m) long single-decks of the 1930s and 1940s, which could have seats for 39, with a squeeze.

Some background on Bristol and Eastern Coach Works might be useful at this point, for their relationship with each other, and with the operators who bought their products, is an important element in the Lodekka story. The Bristol Tramways Company operated its first trams in 1875, and in 1887 became The Bristol Tramways & Carriage Co Ltd, to reflect its expansion into the cab and carriage market. Motor buses were operated from 1906, and only two years later BTCC built its first bus for its own use at Filton, Bristol. In 1912 its expanding Motor Constructional Works was moved to Brislington, and in a short time 'Bristol' chassis were being sold to other customers. BTCC became associated with the Tilling group of bus operators in 1931, and this was the start of a long and close relationship.

In the meantime the growing United Automobile Services fleet, which covered much of the east side of England, opened a maintenance depot in Lowestoft in 1919. In 1920/21 a small coach factory was added, primarily to convert former War Department vehicles, and from 1921/22 new bus bodies were built for the United fleet. In 1929 United became a Tilling & BAT company, and in 1931 the operating area was split, leaving United to concentrate on north-east England. The new Eastern Counties undertaking which took over United's East Anglian operations inherited the United coachworks at Lowestoft, and continued to build bodies there for a growing circle of customers. In 1936 the bodybuilding activities were renamed Eastern Coach Works Ltd, and with Bristol and ECW both under Tilling control, the combination of Brislington and Lowestoft products became increasingly familiar. It was not an exclusive combination, though, nor was it restricted to Tilling fleets. Bristol chassis appeared with other bodies; ECW bodies on other chassis; and municipal, independent and even rival BET group fleets came for the products of both factories.

The main Tilling group single-deck and double-deck models in the immediate prewar and postwar days were the Bristol L and K chassis. The Bristol formula was rather like Guy's — a straightforward sturdy chassis, normally with the Gardner 5LW, a constant mesh gearbox and triple servo brakes. The 6LW Gardner was offered, but rarely specified, until the postwar period, and from 1946 Bristol's own 8.1 litre AVW was available. The AEC 7.7 litre engine first appeared in Bristol K chassis in 1944, and remained available in the early postwar years.

In 1948 the Tilling group, with a large railway shareholding, followed the main-line railway companies into nationalised hands, and passed into the control of the British Transport Commission. Bristol and ECW were also involved in the change of ownership, and under BTC performed a rather different role; apart from the orders outstanding at the time of nationalisation, Bristol and ECW products were restricted to BTC-controlled fleets, and, conversely, these fleets were unable to buy on the open market. By 1949 the Scottish Motor Traction group followed Tilling into BTC hands, but the situation here was slightly different. Within the SMT group was the Alexander bodyworks, which by that time was almost exclusively building for SMT fleets. Upon nationalisation the Alexander coachbuilding interests remained in private hands, although the new Scottish Omnibuses group remained an important customer. The Scottish companies under BTC control were now able to buy Bristol/ECW products, as well as buses available on the open market — the best of both worlds, perhaps. In practice, it was a

The unusual and imposing front end of the first prototype Lodekka LDX, with its extra-wide exposed radiator, and bumper bar. It was new in 1949 to Bristol Tramways, and is seen in 1951 on hire to Hants & Dorset.

A general view of the 1949 prototype, operating on hire to the Westcliff-on-Sea company, showing its unique ECW body style.

The second prototype Lodekka still had the wide exposed radiator, but the ECW body had deeper windows which anticipated the style adopted for production vehicles. Delivered to West Yorkshire in 1950, it is seen here in 1951 on display at the Festival of Britain.

One of the six 1953 pre-production LD6B prototypes operating for Bristol Tramways in Bristol when new. It shows the enclosed radiator and well-proportioned body style, although this slotted style of grille, based on the traditional Bristol design, was not perpetuated

An early production LD6B, supplied to Western National in 1954, with 58-seat ECW body. It is shown here with the slightly revised long grille, which was soon changed to the more familiar shorter shape. It was withdrawn in 1971, and subsequently exported to the USA.

The nationalised Scottish Omnibuses companies also bought Lodekkas in sizeable batches, all with Gardner engines. This 1957 LD6G, with ECW 60-seat body, was new in 1957 to Alexanders, and operated in the maroon livery of its subsidiary David Lawson.

Eastern Counties received six of these long rear-entrance FL6Gs in 1962/63, and one is seen at Peterborough in 1977. It features the neater front grille treatment introduced in 1962.

On its first day in service in May 1959, a Brighton Hove & District LDS, showing the unusual front grille treatment. There were eight LDSs, flat-floor buses which featured Cave-Browne-Cave heating systems, rendering the normal radiator grille opening unnecessary.

The shorter forward-entrance FSF model was less familiar than the FLF. This example was new to Mansfield District in 1961, but had passed to Midland General when seen in Alfreton in 1973 in the distinctive blue which was used in the days before NBC standard liveries took over.

In all-over NBC leaf green, a 1966 Crosville FS6G at Woodside bus station, Birkenhead, in 1974. The white window rubbers favoured by ECW at the time offer some livery relief.

few years before Bristol/ECW buses figured in the Scottish orders, for there was no significant previous history of Bristol or ECW products in Scotland. From the mid-1950s, however, the situation changed, and a good proportion of the double-deck orders came to Bristol/ECW-shared, ironically enough, with the side-gangway lowbridge double-deckers that the Lodekka had rendered largely obsolete.

The two Lodekka prototypes of 1949/50 achieved the low height and normal seating with a split propeller shaft, driving each side of a dropped-centre rear axle; when production Lodekkas followed, these featured a simpler transmission line, consisting of a single offset drive shaft, leading to the offside of a redesigned low-centre back axle. The result was a lower deck floor channel at the same height as the rear platform, and a corresponding reduction in overall height.

The ECW body was semi-integral with the chassis, and had seats for 58. The two prototypes, coded LDX, were 26ft (7.92m) × 7ft 6in (2.28m), and featured unusually wide front radiators; they were supplied to the Bristol and West Yorkshire companies, and during their proving trials also demonstrated to other BTC-associated operators. The mechanical specification was typical Bristol — the AVW engine and constant mesh gearbox.

In 1953 six pre-production prototypes of the Lodekka LD type, featuring the simpler transmission line were built to the legal maximum dimensions of 27ft (8.22m) × 8ft (2.43m). They had enclosed radiators, embodying a representation of the traditional Bristol grille shape, and the ECW body was attractively redesigned, with a less severe front profile, and deep windows on both decks. The body proportions were excellent, and took full account of the inevitable differences in levels between the essentially high driving position and the low-built lower deck. The pre-production LDs were sent to Tilling fleets in different parts of Britain — Bristol, Crosville, Hants & Dorset, United Counties, Western National and West Yorkshire — and full production followed in 1954.

The Lodekka was an instant success, and could soon be found in Tilling and Scottish fleets in growing numbers. In Tilling fashion, the specification was highly standardised; the only real choices were engine — Gardner 5LW or 6LW or Bristol AVW; seating capacity — 58 or 60; open platform or platform doors. The LD5G, with 7 litre Gardner 5LW engine, was favoured by operators with few hills in their territory, like Eastern Counties, Eastern National, Lincolnshire, Thames Valley and United Counties;

Thames Valley also had coach seating in some Lodekkas, as did Central SMT.

The traditional Bristol K chassis remained in production, but the success of the Lodekka hastened its demise in 1957. The LD Lodekka remained in production until 1959, with a few late models entering service in Scotland in 1961; in all 2,179 LDs were built, some later examples with the 8.9 litre Bristol BVW engine, which succeeded the AVW in 1957/58.

Double-deckers were getting bigger at this time, and in 1957 a longer Lodekka appeared, with a 30ft (9.14m) body, with seats for up to 70. Again Bristol followed its eminently sensible custom of building six pre-production buses for service trials before full production began. These buses, coded LDL, went to Tilling fleets for evaluation.

At the same time Bristol engineers were busy improving the breed, and in 1958 produced two prototype Lodekkas featuring a proper flat floor and rear air suspension. Their success led to the appearance of a new family of Lodekkas in 1959. The FS replaced the LD, and the FL the LDL; two new models to cater for the growing interest in the forward-entrance double-decker were the 27ft (8.22m) FSF and 30ft (9.14m) FLF. All featured rear air suspension, and were offered with the Bristol BVW or the Gardner 5LW, 6LW or new 6LX engine.

The FL and FSF models found only a limited market, but the 60-seat FS, and increasingly the 70-seat FLF, were the best sellers. The FS, FL, and FSF latterly disappeared from the model lists, but the FLF continued to enter service in quantity. There was even a slightly longer FLF model, supplied in 1965-67, with a 31ft (9.44m) body which allowed up to 78 seated passengers — equivalent to the rear-engined double-deckers which were becoming increasingly popular — in all but the Tilling fleets.

It could easily be argued that the success of the Lodekka would guarantee a ready market for a bus of this type in the non-nationalised sector. Dennis apparently thought so, and in 1956 announced that agreement had been reached to build and market the Lodekka under licence, as the Loline. A prototype chassis appeared that year, but production did not start until 1958, and continued in fits and starts until 1967. The Dennis Loline, basically a chassis for 30ft (9.14m) bodies, was similar to the Lodekka, but offered Gardner engines as standard, with the further choice of AEC or Leyland engines. The Loline ran to Mk I, Mk II and Mk III versions, but sales were low. Other latter-day Lodekkas like the AEC Bridgemaster and Renown, and the Albion

*Above left:* An early (1957) advert for the Lodekka-based Dennis Loline featured a photo of an ECW-bodied LD Lodekka, retouched with a mock Dennis front end.

*Above:* The Lodekka has been a popular second-hand purchase for independent operators. Hedingham & District, in Essex, bought this 1963 ex-Mansfield District FLF6B 70-seater.

This 1962 FLF6G in the fleet of Scottish Omnibuses was one of the first to feature the revised front end treatment, introduced at the time.

Batches of Lodekka coaches were delivered to several operators over the life of the model. Crosville received five of these FLF6Bs in 1964, with 55-seat ECW bodies suitably modified with extra luggage accommodation. One is seen at Llandudno Junction in 1964, in white and black livery.

Lowlander, suffered a similar fate; at the end of the day less than 300 Loline chassis were built, and it is interesting to speculate how much higher this total surely would have been if the Loline had been available from 1953, as was the Lodekka.

While the Lodekka continued to roll off the production lines, with little more than cosmetic changes to its appearance, there was reorganisation behind the scenes. The manufacturing side of BTCC itself had passed to Bristol Commercial Vehicles in 1955, and in 1957 BTCC itself was retitled, sensibly, Bristol Omnibus Company. The BTC overlords gave way to the Transport Holding Company at the beginning of 1963, and in October 1965 the expanding Leyland Motor Corporation acquired a 25% share in BCV and ECW, which meant that their products could once more be sold on the open market. The result was not a flood of Lodekkas into non-nationalised fleets — ten years previously that might well have been the case. In fact Bristol's excellent rear-engined single-deck model, the RE, was the popular choice, and ECW bodies started to appear on a wider variety of chassis.

There were plans to introduce a separate chassis version of the Lodekka, the LDL model, which would be available for a wider range of bodies. With conventional chassis side-members, the completed vehicle would have been higher than the semi-integral F series models, but the plans for the LDL were dropped.

Later FLF Lodekkas were offered with the option of Leyland engines, and semi-automatic gearboxes, and some operators specified these. But production was running down, and the very last of over 5,000 Lodekkas entered service with Midland General in September 1968. Roughly 1,900 of that total had been FLFs.

The Lodekka's successor was the rear-engined VRL, introduced in prototype form in 1966, with a longitudinally-mounted engine where Leyland and Daimler had plumped for a transverse layout. Production vehicles followed in 1968, but the transverse layout had been adopted, with the code VRT, and few VRLs have been built.

A few Lodekkas are presently preserved, but inevitably as they become thinner on the ground more will be saved. And rightly so, for the sturdy, dependable Lodekka has been a familiar sight on Britain's roads for a quarter of a century.

*Above:* Underneath the arches — a 1966 FLF6G of Mansfield District, in 1975.

*Left:* Many Lodekkas have been converted to open-top for seafront services in holiday resorts; this is 'Lincoln Imp', a 1962 FS6G of Lincolnshire, at Skegness in 1978. It had been new to Brighton Hove & District.

Showing its extra length in the longer rear side windows and rear overhang, an Alexanders (Fife) 1967 FLF6G with 31ft ECW 76-seat body.

*Right:* The classic Leyland Titan PD2 — a 1951 Maidstone & District example seen in 1952 in Lewes. It carried the Farington-style 58-seat Leyland body.

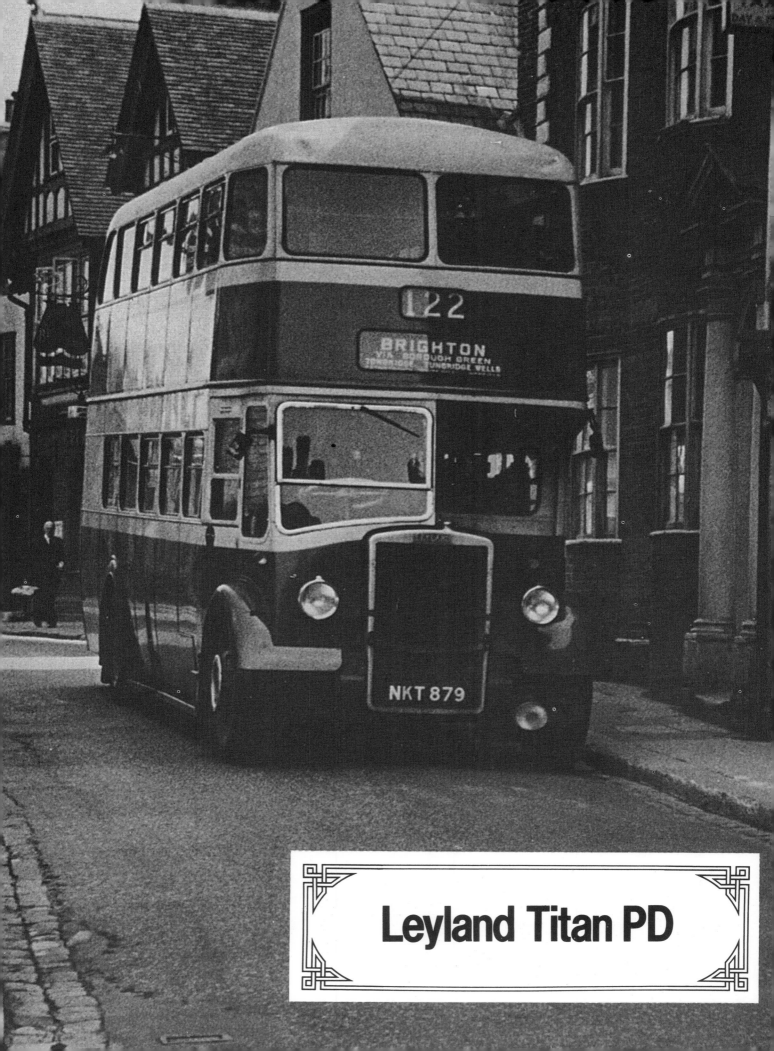

**Leyland Titan PD**

After its enforced disappearance in the war years, Leyland's Titan returned to the model lists in 1946, with the new PD1 model. Here was a double-deck chassis which owed very little to its prewar brothers — unusual at a time when most manufacturers were dusting off prewar designs in the interests of quick resumption of production. It had a new engine, the 7.4 litre E181 unit which had its origins in Leyland's tanks and other military vehicles during the war. With 4-speed constant mesh gearbox and vacuum brakes, production of the PD1 started as soon as possible after the war, late in 1945, and the first bodied examples entered service in 1946.

The PD1 had a short model life, roughly six years, and around 1,500 chassis were built. Its short life was caused by the rapid arrival of its successor, the Titan PD2, in 1947. Looking back, the Titan arrived at just the right time — when postwar loadings were reaching their peak — and its bigger engine and adaptable chassis layout guaranteed it a long and successful life, and an enviable reputation among bus operators.

The bigger engine was the 0.600, which had first been offered in Leyland goods models in 1946; this powerful 9.8 litre unit, working at less than full power, was in the mould of the AEC 9.6 litre of the contemporary Regent Mk III. The 0.600 engine was flexibly mounted, so the PD2 was notably smoother than the PD1, and had a classically solid sound compared with the harsh note of the E181 engine. The standard gearbox was a 4-speed synchromesh unit, and brakes were vacuum assisted.

The PD2 was destined to run to dozens of variants, but at first the options were restricted. The two 1947 models were the PD2/1, suitable for 7ft 6in (2.28m) wide bodies, and the PD2/3, to the newly-legalised 8ft (2.43m) width; both were for bodies to the then current length of 26ft (7.92m). The June 1950 change in permitted vehicle dimension prompted the introduction of the 27ft (8.22m) long PD2/10 and PD2/12 to replace the PD2/1 and PD2/3 chassis. At the same time the air-braked PD2/11 and PD2/13 models joined the lists, although air brakes had previously been available to special order. Following the current trend towards 'new look' full-width fronts, Leyland offered new models from 1953 with a rather anonymous front end structure based on a design first seen on a batch of PD2/12 Titans for Midland Red in 1952.

The basic Titan range now consisted of eight models; four had exposed radiators — two with vacuum brakes, and two with air brakes, in each case to 7ft 6in (2.28m) and 8ft (2.43m) widths; the other four models were the concealed radiator equivalents.

Inevitably not all models sold in large numbers and certain Titans, notably the PD2/12 and equivalent PD2/20, were the most common. Two more variants came in 1955 with the appearance of the pneumo-cyclic gearbox, a semi-automatic epicyclic system which was to become increasingly familiar throughout Britain under different names.

With the legalising of 30ft (9.14m) double deckers in 1956, Leyland extended the PD2's 16ft 5in (5m) wheelbase to 18ft 6in (5.63m) and produced the six Titan PD3 variants — synchromesh and pneumo-cyclic versions, with air or vacuum brakes and concealed or exposed radiators. The PD3's capacity for bigger loads was an immediate attraction; the PD2 had started as a 56-seater, but high seating capacity was all-important in the 1950s, and some operators specified PD2s with up to 66 seats. Now the PD3 offered up to 74 seats.

From 1960 a new style of glass-fibre front end structure was offered in place of the Midland Red-style slotted tin front, and this too had its origins with an operator, in this case St Helens Corporation. The new front was distinctive, and had a family resemblance to current Leyland truck fronts, but it did not persuade some operators to

An early postwar Titan, a Blackburn Corporation PD1 with Leyland body, showing the ornate lining-out and the PD1-style dropped front dash panel.

Outside Newcastle Central station in 1967, two Newcastle Corporation PD2/1 Titans with 56-seat Leyland bodies, new in 1948. The PD2 front dash was shorter than that on the PD1, a useful distinguishing feature.

It was inevitable that the Lancashire municipalities would be faithful Leyland users. Burnley, Colne & Nelson bought many batches of Titans over the years, including 12 of these 1949 all-Leyland PD2/1s.

desert the traditional exposed radiator. Titans with the new front had an 'A' added to their type designation, producing such models as the PD3A/1. The Titan range was rationalised in the 1960s with the disappearance of the little-specified 7ft 6in (2.28m) wide models, and the last of the vacuum-braked chassis.

When the Titan PD2 first appeared it was one of nine double-deck chassis on the British market, and competed with the AEC Regent, Albion Venturer, Bristol K, Crossley DD42, Daimler CV, Dennis Lance, Foden PVD6 and Guy Arab. By the mid-1950s there were really only four chassis in the race — the Regent, CV, Arab and Titan, but important changes were in the air. Leyland's rear-engined Atlantean went into production late in 1958, followed in 1961 by Daimler's Fleetline. Gradually many of the bigger operators drifted away from the conventional front-engined double-deckers and opted for the new rear-engined vehicles. But many others stayed faithful to the Titan for as long as they were able.

The Titan's future now depended on all kinds of influences. The Leyland company was on the verge of spectacular expansion in the early 1960s, taking in arch-rival AEC, and widening into the private car market with its acquisition of Standard-Triumph and Rover. Leyland also engineered a share exchange with the state-owned Bristol and ECW companies, which brought the products of these factories on to the open market for the first time in 17 years.

Jaguar had meantime bought over Daimler and Guy, and then in 1966 the giant BMC empire, to form British Motor Holdings. Some form of merger between these fast-growing combines was inevitable, and in 1968 Leyland took over BMH to create the British Leyland Motor Corporation. Suddenly long-established bus builders who had fought tooth and nail for many years found themselves in a rather uneasy partnership.

Here were the AEC Regent, Bristol Lodekka, Daimler CV, Guy Arab and Leyland Titan, no longer in competition with each other. And there were three rear-engined double-deck models, the Leyland Atlantean, Daimler Fleetline and Bristol VR. Something had to go, and gradually familiar names disappeared from the model lists, until by 1969/70 the front-engined double-decker was no more.

The very last front-engined Titan was a suitably traditional vehicle, ordered by one of the small municipal undertakings in Lancashire which stuck faithfully with Leyland over the years. It was an East Lancs-bodied PD3/14, complete with

exposed radiator, but it was perhaps significant that it was actually delivered to the new Selnec PTE in November 1969, the organisation that had just taken over Ramsbottom UDC, for whom the bus was intended, as well as ten other undertakings in the Greater Manchester area. Little more than nine years later Selnec's successor, Greater Manchester PTE, received the first of its new Titan TN15s, Leyland's 'new generation' double-decker.

These are the bald facts about the Titan PD2 and PD3 chassis, but it is important to look at the bus as it was found in its

76

Leyland also built the bodies on the 500 PD2/3s supplied to London Transport in 1949, although these were to LT design. The chassis were basically PD2s, but had a London variation of the Leyland radiator, and the AEC-type fluid flywheel and preselective gearbox. RTW139 is seen at Victoria in 1952.

Just as the London PD2s were in the minority in an AEC-dominated fleet, Birmingham City Transport's Leylands were outnumbered by Daimlers and Guys. This 1948 PD2/1, seen in 1962, had a 54-seat Brush body.

thousands on the roads of Britain — and indeed *is* to be found on the roads of Britain. Late in 1978, according to the biennial *Commercial Motor* review of major fleets, there were still more than 600 PD2 and PD3 Titans in service with PTE and municipal fleets; and many more have found their way into the hands of independents and contractors, who know a good bus when they see one.

Writing in *Buses*, the noted municipal transport manager Geoffrey Hilditch recalled his first encounter with the Titan PD2:

'My first meeting with a PD2 occurred in the spring of 1948 when I paid a visit to a neighbouring town renowned for its severe operating characteristics. The local undertaking had previously had few Leylands but that very week a handful of new PD2s had been taken into stock and we boarded one of these for a trip to the outer terminal that lay about 1,000ft above the centre and some four miles away. The memory of that ride was not easily effaced. We positively swept up the gradients with the absolute minimum use of the intermediate gears and I was impressed with a bus as I never had been before'.

Praise indeed from a man well known for his

definite views on bus chassis design.

Hilditch ascribed the sales success of the PD2 to two factors — price, which was highly competitive, and the 0.600 engine, of which he wrote: 'This Leyland had the power — 125bhp at 1,800rpm — the torque 410lb/ft at 900rpm — and a surprisingly good specific fuel consumption rate. In addition, although it appeared at a time when the introduction of chromium plated piston rings and detergent oils on a widespread scale were helping to put up mileages between overhauls, it immediately set new life standards thanks to the advanced design adopted.'

Leyland was fond of trade advertisements featuring the Titan's toughness and economy. In 1956 they described how Warrington Corporation had been investigating how far Leyland engines would run without overhaul, and reported how a PD2 had completed 300,000 miles of city working without the head having been removed and was running at 9.73mpg. The next year Leyland was quoting the general manager of Stockton Corporation on the subject of PD2 engines: 'There seems no reason to carry out major overhauls at a fixed mileage, so we confidently expect our engines to reach 400,000 miles, after which each will be kept under careful observation.'

Midland Red received 100 all-Leyland PD2/12s in 1953, and these were fitted with full-width bonnets concealing the radiators; the grille style was adopted as Leyland's standard 'new-look' front, although no more Leyland-bodied vehicles were built with this front.

78

Edinburgh Corporation bought 300 PD2/20s for tram replacement, and fitted them with lightweight Metro-Cammell Orion bodies. The impressive fuel consumption which resulted was featured in Leyland advertising in 1954.

*Above:* Extra cooling grilles were provided on many PD2s, like this 1958 Roe-bodied PD2/30 in the Sheffield City Transport 'A' fleet, seen here when new.

Many operators still preferred the handsome Leyland traditional radiator, as fitted to this 1955 MCW-bodied PD2/13 for Bolton Transport, seen on the Darcy Lever route.

Leigh Corporation required to specify lowbridge or low-height bodies on its double-deckers, and this 1955 PD2/20 had and East Lancs 58-seat body — an all-Lancashire vehicle.

79

Unlike many of its contemporaries, the Titan was not purely a town bus or a country bus; it performed happily on a wide variety of duties, ranging from the most arduous city service work, to inter-urban and rural work for company and independent operators. It could be found in every part of Britain, from Highland Omnibuses in the north, to Plymouth Corporation in the south; it carried bodies by every major coachbuilder in Britain — and a few minor ones too.

Leyland had resumed its own bodybuilding activities after the war with a style on Titan PD1 chassis that owed much to the immediate prewar design on TD7. The sound and well-proportioned lines of this style lasted into the PD2 era; in 1950 an improved version with rubber-mounted windows appeared — the Farington body — and this was further improved to result in one of the most attractive double-deck bodies of all time. Unfortunately Leyland body production ceased in December 1954, although some builders — notably East Lancs and Roe — continued to produce bodies that had the solid traditional look associated with Leyland's.

But solid, traditional bodies were not what was wanted in the weight-obsessed 1950s. This was the era of the ultra-lightweight, and many Titans entered service at this time with bodies which caused traditionalists to hold up their hands in horror. The archetypal lightweight body was the Metro-Cammell Orion, and the most famous Orions were the 300 on Leyland Titan PD2/20 chassis supplied to Edinburgh City Transport in 1954-57 for tram replacement. The bodies were finished to minimum standards, and seats for 63 passengers were fitted into many of the buses. The total unladen weight of Edinburgh's first Orion-bodied Titans was 6 tons 12cwt — of which the body weighed 2 tons 5cwt; these compared with 56-seat all-Leyland PD2/12s of only two years before, which weighed up to 7 tons 18cwt. The weight-saving was mainly in the interests of fuel economy, and Leyland adverts in 1954 revealed that the Edinburgh lightweights were averaging 10.53mpg. But the bodies, although light, were not flimsy, and lasted a full 20 years in hard service.

Leyland was also proud of its order from AEC-dominated London Transport for Titan PD2s which were, in effect, Leyland RTs. Leyland had worked hard to break AEC's near-monopoly of LT supplies, and was rewarded with orders which eventually totalled over 2,000 buses. London had taken virtually standard Titan PD1s in 1946 in the interests of quick delivery, but the order for PD2s called for something very much closer to current London standards. The preselec-

tive gearbox and air brakes of the AEC RT type Regent were specified, and to allow complete body interchangeability the wheelbase was extended. For the 1,631 buses of class RTL built for LT from 1948 Leyland supplied a modified PD2/1, and this received 7ft 6in (2.28m) wide standard RT design bodies by Park Royal, MCW and Weymann. For the 500 RTWs Leyland also supplied the 8ft (2.43m) wide bodies, London's first buses built to this newly-legalised width.

The London buses were not the only preselective Titan PD2s, for Leeds City Transport specified this transmission on ten chassis in 1953, designated PD2/14. Nor were the London RTLs and RTWs the only LT Titans, for it bought eight Titan PD3A/1s in 1962-64 as railway breakdown tender vans.

In addition to the Titans built as Titans, there were several of Leyland's single-deck equivalent, the Tiger, rebuilt and rebodied as double-deckers. West Riding, Yorkshire Traction and Yorkshire Woollen fitted new double-deck bodies to PS1 or PS2 Tigers, as did Barton Transport and Ulster Transport Authority. Alexanders also used Tigers to create new 'Titans', but in a different way. The running units from 17 OPS2 Tigers were fitted in new PD3 chassis frames, and new Alexander lowbridge bodies were fitted to create what the operator christened PD3/3Cs. A conversion of a different type was carried out by Preston Corporation over the years 1959-67. Preston took eight Titan PD2/10s with rear entrance Leyland bodies — some lowbridge — and lengthened the chassis and rebuilt the bodies to 30ft (9.14m) forward-entrance layout; the lowbridge buses were heightened in the process.

The PD2 and PD3 Titans were not built purely for the British market; there were many OPD2s built in left-hand and right-hand drive forms, and PD3s supplied to operators overseas. And the Titan enjoyed a late revival when in 1968 Leyland's Indian subsidiary Ashok Leyland started producing PD3s with 680 engines.

But the Titan PD2 and PD3 were first and foremost British models, in the best traditions of their classic predecessors from Leyland and its rivals. The Titan's passing in 1969 was widely mourned, particularly by engineers who appreciated its reliable, no-nonsense design. Even the Titan could not survive against the combined forces of British Leyland's rationalisation, double-deck one-man operation and the 1968 Transport Act which encouraged rear-engined models in the Bus Grant scheme. In a production life of 22 years around 8,500 PD2s and PD3s had been built, and today more than 70 are preserved, including the inevitable ex-London RTL and RTW examples.

**Above left:** Although the Titan was a popular model in the nationalised Scottish fleets, Scottish Omnibuses only bought 20 new PD2s — and these as an emergency measure. This 1956 PD2/20 had Park Royal lowbridge bodywork, and is seen on service in Glasgow.

**Above:** The PD3 range, suitable for 30ft long bodies, was introduced in 1956. This PD3/1 with Park Royal 74-seat body, was new to Leicester City Transport in 1958.

Another early PD3/1, a 72-seat Burlingham-bodied example supplied to Scout, Preston, in 1958. Like many 30ft double-deckers, it featured a forward entrance.

The revised 'St Helens' style glassfibre front was introduced in 1960, and these two Greater Manchester PD3s demonstrate the differences. HJP 10, a 1961 PD3A/2, has the St Helens front, and GJP 10, a 1960 PD3/2, has the older Midland Red front. These ex-Wigan buses both carried Wigan-built bodies — by Northern Counties and Massey respectively.

81

Although the Scottish Bus Group could (and did) buy Bristol Lodekkas, the lowbridge side-gangway layout was favoured on Leyland Titans until 1961. This PD3A/3 of Western SMT had an Alexander 67-seat bdoy, and is seen in Paisley.

These traditional-looking East Lancs-bodied Titan PD3/14s were from a batch supplied to Stockport Corporation in 1969, and are seen here in Piccadilly, Manchester.

*Left:* The last of Leyland's front-engined Titans was this forward-entrance PD3/14 ordered by Ramsbottom UDC, but delivered to Selnec PTE late in 1969. The 73-seat body was by East Lancs.

*Right:* AEC Reliances on delivery from the Park Royal coachworks in 1960. They were heading north to join the fleet of Venture Transport, of Consett.

The one important phase in the development of the motor bus in Britain which is not represented in this book is the underfloor-engined single-decker. This is not to suggest that there have been no outstanding models, but rather that there has been a less obviously 'classic' design, and the front-runners have been from the AEC and Leyland stables, already well represented in these pages.

In order that the sense of historical balance can be maintained it is of interest to consider briefly the important role played by the underfloor-engined single-decker since the early 1950s. But the story really starts some 20 years earlier, for manufacturers had been working hard to develop successful horizontal engines to release more body space for passenger carrying. The German Büssing firm did much useful pioneering work on flat engines in the 1930s, and in Britain AEC moved towards this layout with the side-engined Q model of 1932. London Transport was a major customer for the AEC Q, and in 1937 developed with Leyland a flat-engined version of the Tiger, and 88 examples were built.

The war slowed development for almost a decade, AEC and Leyland, at least, had produced prototypes for 1939/40, but when peacetime single-deck production resumed in 1945/46, conventional front-engined chassis were chosen. Only Midland Red, producing buses for its own use, plumped wholeheartedly for the underfloor layout with the S6 which went into production in 1946.

It was only a matter of time before the major manufacturers followed suit, and not only the major manufacturers; in fact it was the small Sentinel company which won the race to produce the first commercially-available underfloor-engined vehicles. The big guns were not far behind, though, and in 1949/50 AEC, Atkinson, Dennis, Guy and Leyland all had new underfloor models available. These were generally heavyweight chassis, horizontal-engined versions of the equivalent front-engined models.

Before long most manufacturers added lighter-weight, smaller-engined chassis to their ranges, and these generally took over. Some builders tried to interest British operators in integral — chassisless — single-deckers; there was the AEC/Park Royal Monocoach, the Beadle-Commer, the Harrington Contender and the Leyland/MCW Olympic. Most successful of the integrals in the domestic field was the Bristol/ECW LS, restricted to nationalised operators, but otherwise, separate chassis continued to corner the market.

The underfloor-engined concept was quickly accepted. The absence of engine

intrusion allowed bus bodies with up to 45 seats, and this was readily appreciated by operators seeking maximum capacity. This meant that the previous breed of front-line, front-engined models found few takers; though the front-engined layout did not die on single-deckers, for it survived — and survives — on lighter-weight and smaller-size chassis.

The small engines of the mid-1950s lightweight underfloor single-deckers proved economical, but some operators were looking for greater performance, and bigger engines crept back into the model options. AEC offered the 9.6 litre AH590 engine in its best-selling Reliance as an alternative to the 7.68 litre AH470 and the less popular 6.7 litre AH410.

One of London Transport's 88 trend-setting TF-class coaches, supplied in 1937-39. The chassis was a flat-engined version of the Leyland Tiger, and the majority had 34-seat bodies built by London Transport at Chiswick.

Ribble was an early user of the integrally-constructed underfloor-engined Sentinel/Beadle STC models. Six of these STC4s, 40-seaters with 4-cylinder Sentinel Ricardo engines, were supplied in 1949 and 14 examples of the longer STC6, with 6 cylinder engines, followed in 1951.

London Transport's choice for underfloor-engined chassis was the AEC Regal IV, and its 700-strong RF class was delivered in 1951–53. All had Metro-Cammell bodies, in bus, Green Line coach and private hire coach form. RF370, seen here in 1970 at Bromley-by-Bow, was a red-painted Central Area bus.

The first prototype of the integral Bristol/ECW LS model entered service with Bristol Tramways in 1951. It was a 42-seater with two doors, and had a horizontal Bristol AVW engine. It is seen rounding the Tramway Centre in Bristol when new. The front end styling was unique to the two LSX prototypes.

On hire to London Transport at Reigate in 1953, an early production Bristol/ECW LS5G, which was used on comparison trials with other underfloor models.

85

The Reliance chassis had first appeared in 1953 along with the Monocoach, which was mechanically similar although offered as an integral bus with Park Royal body. Operators were quick to order the Reliance, and it figured in BET, SBG, municipal and independent fleets throughout Britain. In 1961 a 36ft (11m) Reliance was added to the range and in 1968, following another change in regulations, a 39ft 4in (12m) chassis appeared. The trusty 470 and 590 engines were replaced by new 505 and 690 units, and the 690 itself was replaced by the 761 engine — all 12.47 litres of it. Originally the Reliance was available with a choice of vacuum or air braking systems, but latterly air brakes were standard. Similarly there had been a choice of synchromesh gearboxes, though more recent Reliances have featured the German ZF box. Leaf springs have been standard, with a coil springing option introduced in 1967.

With the closure of AEC's Southall works the Reliance was withdrawn from the models lists after an amazing 25 year run. A constant seller throughout its life, the Reliance was latterly a popular choice for heavy-duty coaching work, although Leyland's Leopard had overtaken it as the most popular chassis in this range.

Leylands's first excursion into underfloor single-deckers was the Tiger FEC for London Transport in 1937; in 1948 a production underfloor model was announced, the Leyland/MCW Olympic, a complete chassisless bus. The integral concept was not popular with British operators, and while the Olympic sold well in the export market, a new separate chassis, the Royal Tiger, appeared in 1950. The sturdy Royal Tiger, with 9.8 litre 0.600 engine, was joined in 1952 by the Tiger Cub, with the 5.86 litre 0.350 engine, and like AEC's Reliance most customers chose the smaller-engined bus. The engine was not always sufficiently powerful for some of the more demanding Tiger Cub duties, and it was progressively uprated to become the 6.54 litre 400 unit. This was still not enough for some operators; some took the Royal Tiger Worldmaster chassis, primarily an export model, but a demand for a lighter-weight chassis with a big engine produced the Leopard in 1959. The 600-engined Leopard proved an ideal chassis for stretching when 36ft (11m) vehicles were legalised in 1961; after this the Leopard really took off.

From 1966 the big 11.1 litre 680 engine was an option, and from 1973 it became the standard fitment. The Leopard was available from the start with a choice of synchromesh or pneumo-cyclic semi-automatic gearboxes, though the semi-automatic box steadily became the more popular option; interest from the Scottish Bus Group produced a Leopard with ZF synchromesh gearbox, and this became a general option with the disappearance of the Reliance in 1979.

The Reliance and Leopard have been the two most notable 'own-engine' underfloor single-deckers. Several other builders fitted the horizontal Gardner engines, traditional favourites with many operators. Most numerous were the Bristol models, the LS and MW — although the LS was also available with Bristol's own AVW unit. Other Gardner-engined models came from Atkinson, Daimler and Guy, but in smaller numbers; Daimler also offered a horizontal version of its 10.6 litre CD650 engine in its Freeline chassis. Another maker to use proprietary units was Bristol with the light LH model, offered with Leyland or Perkins engines.

A late entry in the underfloor market was the Seddon Pennine 7, developed jointly with the Scottish Bus Group; it was first seen in 1973 and featured a Gardner 6HLXB engine and ZF synchromesh gearbox, although later models featured semi-automatic and fully-automatic boxes. In spite of the Gardner engine, it was not a big seller outside the SBG; the Leopard had become the popular choice for heavyweights, and many independents stuck to the Bedford/Ford ranges, which had progressed from the days when they were regarded primarily as light-weight vehicles. Bedfords and Fords grew with the legal dimensions, and as the chassis grew, so did the engines.

After sticking firmly to the front-engined layout, Bedford changed to a mid-engined underfloor layout in 1970 with its new YRQ model; unusually, the engine — a 7.6 litre Bedford 466 unit — was mounted *vertically* under the floor. The YRQ was joined by the 36ft (11m) YRT in 1972, and these were replaced by the bigger-engined YLQ/YMT in 1975, with the 8.2 litre 500 unit.

Ford resisted the underfloor layout, but in 1977 tilted the front-mounted turbo 360 5.9 litre engine to overcome criticisms of engine intrusion and noise at the front door.

The rear-engined single-decker inherited much of the service bus work from the underfloor models in the late 1960s, and rightly so, for the inherent problem with the underfloor layout has always been the essentially high steps and floor line. But for inter-urban, express and touring work the underfloor-engined models have a bright future, and Leyland is revamping its trusty Leopard to incorporate a more up-to-date specification, which will undoubtedly increase its appeal and lengthen its lifespan.

In 1954 Sheffield Transport bought two of these unusual Leyland/MCW Olympics with 31-seat standee bodies, featuring the Scottish-type cut-away rear entrance.

The Leyland Royal Tiger was a popular choice for many fleets, including the former Great Northern Railway (Ireland), which had a number of these Saunders-Roe bodied 44-seaters; one of them is seen between Dublin and Drogheda.

The integral AEC/Park Royal Monocoach was considerably less successful than the Reliance chassis, although several fleets in Scotland and northern England bought sizeable batches. This 1955 Scottish Omnibuses example, seen in Edinburgh in 1955, was one of 95 Monocoaches delivered between 1954-57, including some later vehicles with Alexander bodies.

The Freeline was Daimler's only underfloor-engined model, and three of these Freeline coaches with Willowbrook 41-seat bodies were delivered to Coventry Corporation in 1959.

*Right:* The Reliance was particularly successful in coach form, and these photographs show (*main picture*) a 1968 Plaxton example for Galleon Tours, in the Scottish highlands; (*inset, upper*) a 1962 East Kent example with Park Royal body in Skyways livery — these chassis were later rebodied; (*inset lower*) a pair of 1964 Harrington Grenadier-bodied Reliances delivered to BOAC for coach services between Glasgow and Prestwick Airport.

*Left:* Midland Red built its CM5 class in 1959 to operate Birmingham-London express services on the new M1 motorway. They had 8 litre turbocharged underfloor engines, and were capable of 85mph. The coaches seen here were CM5Ts, with 34-seat bodies which featured toilet accommodation.

The AEC Reliance found a new lease of life in its 36ft form, and this North Western example was one of 20 Willowbrook-bodied 51-seat examples delivered in 1963.

The Leyland Leopard became very much a Scottish Bus Group standard single-decker in the 1960s and 1970s, the vast majority with Alexander Y type bodies. This 49-seater was new for Western SMT in 1968, and is seen in Edinburgh.

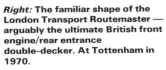

*Right:* The familiar shape of the London Transport Routemaster — arguably the ultimate British front engine/rear entrance double-decker. At Tottenham in 1970.

A more unusual Leopard/Y type was Edinburgh Corporation 101, a three-door standee bus dating from 1961. The rear entrance doors led to a wide platform, and passengers paid a seated conductor; the two other doors were for exit only.

The Leopard has also been a popular choice for National Bus Company orders, and this 1972 Leopard/Duple coach in the National Travel (South West) fleet is seen leaving Cheltenham coach station in 1976.

# AEC Routemaster

Whether or not the London Transport Routemaster was 'probably the greatest step forward in bus design not only in London Transport's history but for the bus world in general', as one writer has suggested, is a matter of opinion. Certainly it deserves a place in this book as one of the most remarkable buses of postwar years and a worthy successor to the legendary RT.

The Routemaster was initially conceived as a replacement for London Transport's large trolleybus fleet. It was to be a completely new vehicle, in no way derived from AEC's current Regent chassis. In fact it was conceived as a complete vehicle jointly by London Transport, AEC and Park Royal; it was to be an integral bus, with no separate chassis, and would consist of a sub-frame plus an aluminium alloy body. LT engineers had developed a hydraulic braking system and an independent suspension system, and these were incorporated in the first prototype, unveiled in 1954.

This was RM1, 'London's Bus of the Future' with AEC 9.6 litre engine and fully-automatic transmission. At 27ft (8.22m) × 8ft (2.43m) it was bigger than the RT, and offered 64 seats against the RT's 56; yet it weighed 6 ton 14cwt, compared with 7 ton 5cwt of the RT. The handsome rear-entrance body was built at LT's Chiswick Works, and was in many ways a modernised RT, with the well balanced and deceptively subtle timeless lines of that design. An unusual full-width front end was fitted, featuring a prominent LT 'bullseye' logo; this did not last long, and a more normal front grille was fitted when in 1956 the radiator was moved from its former position under the driver's cab.

A second prototype, RM2, followed in 1955. It was basically similar to RM1, but at first had the smaller AV470 engine, and worked in London Transport's Country Area. RML3 came next, built by Weymann and featuring a Leyland 0.600 engine. This engine was also fitted in CRL4, built by Eastern Coach Works as a 57-seat Green Line coach.

The four prototypes entered service between 1956 and 1958, and further experience was gained by running two sets of production RM components fitted out as lorries, in service conditions. Production Routemasters did not start to appear until early 1959 — nearly four years after the debut of RM1. In these five years the size and shape of the double-deck bus had gone through a fairly major change; from July 1956 double-deck buses could be up to 30ft (9.14m) long, and late in 1958 the first examples of Leyland's trend-setting rear-engined Atlantean were entering service.

London was committed to the RM, however, and production vehicles from the first batch of 850 entered trial service on various routes in the summer of 1959. The first major RM debut took place in November 1959 when new buses started to replace trolleybuses, and this continued until the closure of LT's trolleybus system in 1962; after this the RM was used to replace RTs. All production Routemasters carry Park Royal bodies, and most had the new AEC AV590 9.6 litre engine.

The production RMs, shorter than the permitted maximum, with front engines and open rear platforms, might have been regarded as something of an anachronism late in 1959 when they first entered service in any quantity, yet they had advanced technical features like hydraulic brakes, independent front suspension and rear air suspension that are still far from commonplace more than 20 years later. And the combination of compact length and punchy engine made the RM ideal for London traffic conditions.

But longer Routemasters were soon to follow, by slotting an extra short bay into the body sides; there were 24 RMLs delivered in 1961, with seats for 72.

These were not the only odd examples, for the RM story was one of constant development. There was RM664, delivered in 1961 in a special unpainted aluminium finish, which it carried until 1965; RMF1254, a 69-seat forward-entrance Routemaster, exhibited at the 1962 Commercial Motor Show, which never entered LT service because of union opposition, and spent some years on demonstration duties and running with British European Airways, before acquisition by Northern General Transport. Mention of BEA and Northern General is a reminder that these were the only non--London Transport customers for the Routemaster when it came on general sale, marketed by Park Royal. In 1964/65 Northern General bought 50 long forward entrance Routemasters, similar to RMF1254, but with Leyland 600 engines. (In fact Northern also bought RMF1254 — still unused in service by LT — and fitted a 600 engine). These were enthusiastically received and the Routemaster's inherent sophistication was greatly appreciated. In *Bus & Coach* for May 1965 William Lambden wrote:

'Much of the territory covered by the Routemasters is subject to subsidence because of mining activities. Consequently road surfaces are often bad. In fact, Northern General has always had to face the risk of getting more spring damage than the average operator. Therefore the special

The 1954 prototype Routemaster, RM1, with its original front, in its first few weeks of service in 1956, at Crystal Palace.

Routemasters are prepared for trolleybus replacement duties at Poplar Garage in November 1959. The buses have the original style of radiator and heater grilles, and bodies without opening windows at the front of the upper deck.

Coach Routemasters. RMC1456 (*left*) at Marble Arch in 1963, and a 1962 advert for the same vehicles (*below left*). The prototype Routemaster coach, with ECW body, is seen (*below*) in its original guise as CRL4. The RMCs were downgraded to bus duties by London Country, and RMC1463 is seen (*bottom*) in NBC green at Berkhamsted in 1976.

PARK ROYAL forward entrance Routemaster, with A.E.C. running units, in service with British European Airways.

## PARK ROYAL°—ROE
### *Sales Division*

HEAD OFFICE AT:
**PARK ROYAL VEHICLES LTD**
ABBEY ROAD. LONDON. N.W. 10
PRV

ROE

*Above left:* A contemporary advert for the Routemaster, marketed by Park Royal, featuring one of the BEA vehicles in its original livery.

*Above:* Northern General was the other Routemaster user, and in 1966 added an extra vehicle to its 50 1964/65 vehicles. This was the former London Transport RMF1254 (*right*) — which had not been operated by LT — which joined the similar Northern buses, represented by 2122 on the left.

A BEA Routemaster at Heathrow in 1972 carrying the later orange and white corporate livery, and showing the Marshall-built luggage trailer.

In its ultimate blue and white British Airways livery, this bus became London Transport RMA44, for staff bus duties.

independent coil springing arrangements of the Routemaster are proving highly satisfactory. On bad roads the bus tends to pitch a little more than those with orthodox leaf springs, or with air springing, but there is a noticeable absence of roll at either high or low speeds. When the first bus went into service Northern General obtained local publicity by its claim that special suspension arrangements gave riding characteristics akin to the private car. That claim has been justified by results obtained on the sub-standard roads.

'Drivers welcomed the power-assisted steering, and were quick to learn its use when undergoing special spells of instruction before taking out a Routemaster on service. They were at first, however, not quite so quick to appreciate the techniques of the two-stage Lockheed hydraulic brakes, another of the special features of the London Transport specification.'

BEA chose 65 forward entrance short 27ft 6in (8.38m) Routemasters for its Heathrow Airport-Gloucester Road Air Terminal service in 1966/67, operated with luggage trailers. The bigger AEC AV690 11.3 litre engine was fitted. BEA's 65 buses, plus Northern's 50, represented the only non-LT Routemasters.

In the meantime London's own RMs were entering service at a rate of around 300 a year. Apart from the 24 long buses, London stuck to the 27ft 6in (8.38m) variant, including a batch of 68 Green Line coaches delivered in 1962; these had 57 coach seats and rear platform doors, and were coded RMC. Around this time several hundred RMs entered service with Leyland 600 engines.

From 1965 production for London Transport switched to 30ft (9.14m) rear-entrance Routemasters, starting with a batch of 43 long Green Line coaches, 65-seaters coded RCL. There followed 500 RML buses, including 100 for the Country Area, concluding with the delivery of RML2760 in 1968 — nine years after the first production vehicles appeared, and 14 years after RM1's debut. The end of the RM production — 'cut in the prime of life' according to one writer — was the result of several factors.

A major report, *Reshaping London's Bus Services*, appeared in 1966, recommending several solutions to the problems of traffic congestion, staffing difficulties and passenger decline that were seriously affecting services. This heralded a wholesale switch to single-deckers, and large purchases of proprietary

London Routemasters have worn a wide variety of special liveries. For the 1977 Silver Jubilee celebrations, 25 RMs were painted silver, with a red band, and renumbered SRM1-25. SRM7 (RM1871) is seen at Piccadilly.

A selection of Routemasters in advertising liveries, for Sharp, Hanimex and Pye. The Hanimex bus is an RML variant, 30ft with the 'extra' window in the centre of the side.

*Above:* For the 150th anniversary of the 1829 introduction of the Shillibeer horse bus, 12 RMs received this green, red and yellow 'Omnibus' livery, as worn by RM2153 in Euston Road in 1979.

In 1979 15 RMs received the red and yellow Shoplinker livery for an unsuccessful West End shoppers' service.

97

AEC chassis that were to prove far from successful in London conditions.

There had been relatively unsuccessful forays into the rear-engined field with LT's experimental batches of Leyland Atlanteans and Daimler Fleetlines in 1965, and there was FRM1, the rear-engined Routemaster, which could well have been the first of a large fleet.

FRM1, completed in 1966, was developed by LT, AEC and Park Royal as a natural development of the highly-successful Routemaster concept. Ingenious design resulted in an integral double-decker with an AEC AV690 engine mounted transversely at the rear, and a high proportion of standard RM parts. Sadly FRM1 remained unique, and in such a highly-standardised fleet has never settled in really suitable duties.

London's next double-deckers were to be 2,646 Daimler Fleetlines, delivered between 1970 and 1978, but these only confirmed LT's belief that 'off the peg' buses are not suited to London conditions, and the Routemasters, in some cases 20 years older than the Fleetlines, are expected to outlive them in LT service.

Although Routemaster deliveries were completed in 1968, interest in the type did not stop there. In 1969 RM1737 became the first British bus to carry an all-over advertisement (for Silexine Paints), at the start of the recent craze for this style of advert. In 1970 the LT Country Area became a new National Bus Company subsidiary, London Country Bus Services, and 209 Routemasters passed to the new fleet. In 1973 the top deck of RM1368 was burned out, and the bus was converted to a single-decker and retained for research purposes by LT's Chiswick Works.

The LT Routemaster fleet was augmented in 1975 by the acquisition of 13 of the British Airways (ex-BEA) vehicles; these were classed RMA, and after a short spell in passenger service were switched to driver tuition and staff duties. A further 14 RMAs followed in 1976, and following the closure of the Gloucester Road terminal the remainder of the former BEA vehicles came to LT.

More Routemasters came to London Transport in 1977-79 — or more precisely came *back* — for London Country decided to withdraw its fleet of RMCs, RCLs and RMLs, and LT agreed to buy them. Although several were withdrawn and sold for scrap, many RMLs re-entered LT service after overhaul, and many of the RMC and RCL vehicles were retained by LT as staff or driver trainer vehicles.

Routemasters were chosen in 1977 when 25 vehicles were painted in special silver

livery to mark the Queen's Silver Jubilee, and these were temporarily renumbered SRM1-25. In a similar exercise in 1979, 12 RMs were repainted into a green, red and cream 'Omnibus' livery to mark the 150th anniversary of Shillibeer's pioneering horse bus service in London.

At the same time, those who thought that 2760 would be the highest numbered Routemaster in London were confused by the appearance of vehicles carrying numbers from RMF2761 upwards in 1978/79. The explanation was a simple one; these were ex-Northern General vehicles, hired to LT for the Round London Sightseeing Tour, and painted — and numbered — accordingly.

Further confusion was created by *yet more* Routemasters numbered from RMF 2761, which appeared in 1980. These were genuine LT buses, however, acquired from Northern General.

So the Routemaster story goes on. With the oldest vehicles more than 20 years old — but revitalised regularly after every one of LT's thorough overhauls — there is no sign of the class disappearing from London's streets. The Routemaster — surely the ultimate expression of the traditional British front engine/rear entrance double-decker, is set to soldier on in the front line well into the 1980s, maintaining the standards of its illustrious forebear, the RT.

**Northern General Routemasters started to appear in London in 1978, firstly for spares and in 1979 for service with London Transport. This is one of two owned by Brakell, Cheam, and hired to LT for the Sightseeing Tour. In LT colours, with LT-style destination display, it was actually numbered 'RMF2761'.**

*Right:* **One of the first four production Leyland Atlanteans, a Metro-Cammell-bodied bus for Wallasey Corporation, seen on its first day in service, late in 1958. The rear view shows the controversial engine bustle which the Atlantean introduced to the British streets.**

# Leyland Atlantean

The Leyland name figures strongly in the development of the British double-decker, and just as the Titan TD1 heralded a whole new breed of low-built, big-engined buses, so the Leyland Atlantean in 1956 set a pattern that has not really changed since that time. True, chassis like the Daimler COG6, AEC RT and Bristol Lodekka added further refinements to the TD1 concept, culminating, as we have seen, in the London Routemaster; but the Atlantean pioneered the now almost universal practice of mounting the engine transversely at the rear of the chassis, permitting a front overhang and an extreme front entrance.

Not that rear engines were particularly new. By the early 1950s they were fairly common overseas, particularly in the United States, and even in Britain the layout was not completely unknown. In 1935/36 Midland Red built four experimental rear-engined buses, with petrol-engines coupled to fluid flywheels and epicyclic gearboxes. And in 1938 London Transport bought 49 rear-engined Leyland Cubs, its CR class, which had a chequered career. At this time though, there was more interest in developing flat underfloor engines for single-deckers, and war set progress back for a decade. In 1950 Foden, traditionally a truck builder, introduced the rear-engined PVR6 single-deck model, and in 1956 there followed the Rutland Clipper — but neither chassis was a significant success.

Leyland's experimental department at this time was dabbling with several concepts, including rear-mounted engines, epicyclic gearboxes, small turbo-charged engines, and integral construction. Most of these were unpopular ideas with staunchly traditional British busmen, and it took many years before Leyland succeeded in producing a successful vehicle incorporating all these features — in fact the Leyland National of 1970 was probably the first.

But in its desire to evaluate new ideas in 1952 Leyland built an experimental double-deck chassis which was first publicly shown outside the 1954 Commercial Motor Show. Christened the Low-Loader, it had a Saunders-Roe 61-seat body with a flat, almost trolleybus-like, front. The engine, a turbocharged 5.76 litre 0.350 unit, was mounted at the rear, literally on the rear open platform; a preselective gearbox was fitted and there was independent front suspension. The overall height was only 13ft 3in (4.03m).

The Low-Loader was used as a demonstrator by several operators, and Leyland monitored its progress. A second vehicle was built in 1955, with a similar chassis (but with a pneumo-cyclic gearbox) and a Metro-Cammell body of slightly more conventional

appearance, incorporating the familiar double-deck half-cab arrangement. Both buses passed to the Glasgow independent Lowland Motorways in 1957, but when Scottish Omnibuses took over the Lowland business at the end of the same year, they were not involved in the sale, and were destined to lead varied careers. The second prototype, XTC684, is preserved.

From experience with these buses, Leyland set about designing an improved vehicle. The legalising of 30ft (9.14m) double-deckers in 1956 gave the final boost, and for the 1956 London Show Leyland and MCW had produced the semi-integral Atlantean prototype, 281 ATC. This bus introduced the familiar set-back front axle and front entrance, with the engine at the rear — and the big 9.8 litre 0.600 unit was chosen after all.

*Top:* **The Low-Loader with its trolleybus-like Saunders-Roe body, featured a small turbocharged engine mounted on the rear platform. It was demonstrated to several operators in the early 1950s including Ulster Transport Authority, as seen here.**

**The second PDR1 prototype, built in 1954, had a Metro-Cammell body, and a front end treatment similar to that on London's TF coaches (see page 84). It is now preserved.**

Leyland and MCW had managed to produce a low-height bus — 13ft 3in (4.03m) — with normal seating on both decks, and a pneumo-cyclic gearbox. This prototype was used by several operators, but semi-integral construction and air suspension were not popular features, and the Atlantean was relaunched in production form late in 1958.

Now the Atlantean, coded PDR1/1, was offered as a separate chassis with leaf springs, and any bodybuilder could complete the vehicle. Most common of the Atlanteans were the normal height 14ft 6in (4.41m) versions, seating up to 78; but an unusual semi-lowbridge version was available, 13ft 4in (4.06m) high, with lowbridge-type side gangway and four-abreast seats at the rear of the upper deck. Sales of the Atlantean were slow at first, and many major operators stuck firmly to their normal front-engined chassis, although often in 30ft (9.14m) forward-entrance form. Gradually the Atlantean became a familiar sight in many parts of Britain, and the Ribble group created a great deal of interest in 1959 with its first Gay Hostess, a double-deck coach based on Leyland Atlantean chassis. The normal, rather box-like, MCW body was specified, but fitted out with 50 reclining seats, and toilet and kitchen accommodation, for opera-

tion on the first of Britain's motorways which were then opening. To maintain the motorway speeds, a bigger engine, the 11.1 litre 680 unit, was fitted, and this was an option for some years, eventually becoming a standard Atlantean fitment.

Before long the Atlantean had a rival. Daimler announced its rear-engined Fleetline model in 1960, and it went into full production two years later. The layout of the Fleetline was similar to that of the Atlantean, but it featured a drop-centre rear axle which permitted low height bodies with normal seating throughout, and it had the Gardner 6LX engine, a firm favourite with many operators.

It is fair to say that the early Fleetline was a better bus than the early Atlantean, but both models settled down with a growing list of orders. Leyland tried to counter some of the Fleetline's attractions with the PDR1/2 Atlantean in 1964, featuring the drop-centre double reduction rear axle of the Albion Lowlander and thus offering a true low-height vehicle — but with limited success.

The turning-point in the story of the rear-engined double-decker came in 1966 when one-man double deckers were legalised, and while some operators adapted front-engined vehicles for OMO, the Atlantean/Fleetline

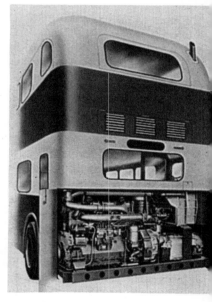

The 1956 integral Atlantean, 281 ATC, whose attractive Metro-Cammell body set a design trend for all future rear-engined double-deckers. The thick side window pillars were for structural reasons. The drawing of the rear end shows the original style of engine compartment, and a proposed roof-level exhaust system which was not adopted.

had obvious advantages over them. The same year heralded the appearance of two new rear-engined models.

First was the rear-engined London Transport Routemaster, which was to have been the first of several prototypes produced by AEC for general sale. As we have seen, this never happened — perhaps because Leyland had taken-over AEC in 1962, and Leyland was in the process of expansion and rationalisation. Leyland had also, of course, bought into Bristol and ECW, which brought these makers back on to the open market. The nationalised Tilling and Scottish fleets were still buying Lodekkas, but a new rear-engined Bristol was on the way. It appeared as the VRL in 1966, with Gardner 6LX engine mounted longitudinally in the rear offside corner, but this layout was not a popular one, and most production Bristol VRs have been VRT models with transverse engine.

Leyland continued to grow and in 1968 bought out BMH to create British Leyland; every builder of double-deck vehicles was now Leyland-controlled. The combined effects of Leyland's expansion, double-deck OMO, and major changes in the bus industry following the 1968 Transport Act, did much to help the Atlantean, and helped to kill the remaining front-engined double-deckers.

The result was a restricted choice, with only the Atlantean, Fleetline and VR available by 1970. Longer Atlanteans were offered from 1966, coded PDR2/1, but it was becoming clear that the basic concept of the vehicle was showing its age; there had been constant improvements, but the chassis was now 12 years old.

The industrial troubles of the early 1970s, and the infamous three-day week, aggravated the situation, and created problems for Leyland, for bodybuilders and for customers. The first break in Leyland's monopoly came in 1973 when two new double-deck models were introduced. There was the Metropolitan, built by Metro-Cammell using a rear-mounted Scania engine and other running units; and the Ailsa, developed in Scotland using a *front*-mounted Volvo engine. In desperation many operators turned to these models in an effort to guarantee quicker deliveries.

On the bright side, though, Leyland had introduced a revised Atlantean model in 1972, coded AN68.1 (9.5m) and AN68.2 (10m). The AN68 was a great improvement on the previous range, allowing increased passenger circulation space, better engine cooling and several safety features based on experience with the PDR variants.

Over 6,000 PDR Atlanteans had been built in its 14-year life, and while most had

At the 1958 Commercial Show, a low-height Atlantean/MCW for James, Ammanford, the former BET subsidiary.

been fairly conventional vehicles, there were some non-standard versions. Great Yarmouth and Portsmouth Corporations fitted the Atlantean chassis with single-deck bodywork, a move towards greater standardisation; operators also did this with the Daimler Fleetline, which was actually offered as a single-deck vehicle. Another unusual Great Yarmouth batch of Atlanteans were double-deckers built to a restricted length of 28ft (8.52m). Then there were the 36ft 4.5in (11.07m) Atlanteans for Stockholm in 1967, built at the time when Sweden was changing the rule of the road.

The Fleetline had been suffering from a shortage of Gardner engines, and from 1970 Leyland engines were offered. Then in 1973 Fleetline production was switched from Coventry to Leyland to allow greater space for car production. This too caused a production hiccup, but soon both chassis were being built in close proximity, and eventually the Leyland name was applied to the Fleetline.

Further competitors appeared on the double-deck scene in the mid-1970s with the introduction of the Foden-NC and Dennis Dominator, aimed at the Fleetline market. Leyland had by this time announced details of its advanced new-generation B15 double-

decker, later christened Titan, and MCW was well advanced in the development of the Metrobus, with Gardner or Rolls-Royce engine.

It had been Leyland's declared intention to phase out the long-running Atlantean/Fleetline/VR triumverate when the new Titan was in full production, but delays at Park Hotel, and a continuing demand for the 'old generation' chassis ensured a prolonged model life. At the end of the day the Atlantean had shaken off its early reputation, and in its AN68 form was widely regarded as the best model of its type.

Certainly there are large fleets of satisfied Atlantean customers throughout Britain. Many are PTE fleets, like Greater Glasgow, which received its 1,000th Atlantean with due ceremony in 1975; Greater Manchester, with a huge fleet of over 1,100 (and over 900 Fleetlines); Merseyside with 900-plus, West Yorkshire with around 500, South Yorkshire with 360 and Tyne & Wear with 300. Other large municipal users included Lothian (500 plus), Nottingham (225), Hull (204) and Grampian, Plymouth, Portsmouth and Southampton, each with over 100.

Atlanteans are thinner in the nationalised sector, where the Bristol VRT has been the standard double-deck model, but several fleets have been able to take new Atlanteans, and these have usually been former BET fleets with a strong Leyland tradition, like Northern General, Ribble and Southdown, while former Tilling fleets like Hants & Dorset and Western National have received older Atlanteans to speed one-man conversions; London Country, which inherited a fairly elderly fleet from London Transport, has received more than 200 Atlanteans to help replace RTs and Routemasters. Scottish Bus Group has never bought Atlanteans new, and has preferred the Daimler Fleetline, to overcome its low bridge problem.

And the Atlantean can be found in many different situations overseas. There are Atlantean fleets in Eire, Portugal, South Africa, Iran, Iraq, India and Australia, and a notable order was for eight Park Royal-bodied AN68.2Ls for service in New York.

The Leyland Atlantean, first of the rear-engined double-deckers, looks set to be the last of the 'old generation' models in production, to judge from the significant orders which, at the time of writing, are still coming in from operators who prefer to stick with the tried and tested AN68 for as long as they can before venturing into the unknown and the new-generation models.

The first attempt to improve the box-like looks of the bodywork on Atlantean chassis was made by Liverpool Corporation. For a large order delivered from 1962, these attractive Metro–Cammell bodies were specified, and three are seen in central Liverpool in 1970.

Manchester Corporation was another large Atlantean user, and its distinctive Mancunian bodies were designed for one-man operation. Two new PDR2/1s with Park Royal 76-seat bodies are seen in Piccadilly in 1969.

In deceptively rural surroundings, one of the Standerwick Gay Hostess Atlantean coaches at 50mph on the M1 in 1960. Weymann built the 50-seat bodies, which included reclining seats, kitchen and toilet.

Few operators specified single-deck Atlanteans, and 12 of these PDR2/1s with Seddon 40-seat bodies were supplied to Portsmouth Corporation in 1971. One is seen at Southsea in 1977.

Independent operators have also specified Atlanteans, like this attractive AN68/2R with Northern Counties 82-seat body in the fleet of Delaine, of Bourne. It is painted in the unusual two-tone blue and cream livery.

*Below left:* London Transport ordered 50 Atlanteans in 1965, and fitted them with Park Royal bodies to a most uninspired design. XA2 is seen in Parliament Square when new.

*Above:* A 1973 AN68/1R in the fleet of the former independent operator Cunningham of Paisley, fitted with Alexander 72-seat body. At the Paisley terminus on the last night of operation in 1979.

*Far left:* A 1961 Leyland advert featuring the first of Glasgow's huge fleet of Alexander-bodied Atlanteans.

*Left:* A 1962 advert for the MkII Atlantean, with a Liverpool Corporation Metro-Cammell example.

*Above left:* Atlanteans have been equally popular in several overseas cities. This is one of a large fleet for Singapore Bus Services, here with Metal Sections body.

*Above:* Baghdad Passenger Transport Services operates a large fleet of these rugged-looking AN68/2Ls with Park Royal bodies.

*Left:* Eight Atlanteans, with Park Royal bodies based on the Manchester Mancunian design, were built for New York in 1976.

*Below:* Earlier exported Atlanteans were the 50 36ft long buses supplied to Stockholm Tramways in 1967. These imposing buses had Park Royal bodies.

*Right:* Probably the ultimate rear-engined single-deck chassis — the Bristol RELL, here with ECW two-door bus body, in the Bristol Omnibus fleet, in home-town Bristol.

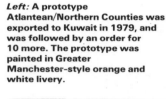

*Left:* A prototype Atlantean/Northern Counties was exported to Kuwait in 1979, and was followed by an order for 10 more. The prototype was painted in Greater Manchester-style orange and white livery.

# Bristol RE

One of the unhappiest chapters in the recent history of the bus concerned the rear-engined single-deck chassis. As we have seen, the underfloor-engined single-decker dominated the large British fleets in the 1950s, and Leyland's Atlantean double-decker spearheaded a massive move to rear engines. A rear engine in a single-deck chassis was not new; it had been tried by Midland Red and London Transport in the 1930s and Foden in the 1950s, but without notable success.

When 36ft (11m) vehicles were legalised in 1961 high-capacity single-deckers suddenly became even more attractive as an alternative to double-deckers. Up to 54 seated passengers could be carried comfortably, with, in some cases, space for 24 theoretical standees — more than equal in total to most double-deckers. In addition one-man double-deckers had not yet been authorised, and high-capacity single-deckers were an acceptable option for most operators, but there was the drawback that the high floor levels of underfloor-engined chassis inhibited easy passenger access. The solution seemed to be a horizontal engine mounted behind the rear axle, and the first British chassis to develop this layout was the one which is remembered as undoubtedly the best; the Bristol RE.

The magazine *Bus & Coach* had long been an advocate of the advantages of a rear-engined single-decker, and when the RE chassis was unveiled in 1962, technical editor P. M. A. Thomas sagely remarked: 'It may well mark the beginning of a new phase in British passenger vehicle design.'

The relationship between Bristol, Eastern Coach Works and the British Transport Commission bus fleets has already been covered, and the new RE chassis was only available to nationalised undertakings. Bristol's existing single-deck model was the MW, a conventional 30ft (9.14m) long chassis with underfloor-mounted Gardner engine. Unlike AEC and Leyland, Bristol had not chosen to meet the new 36ft (11m) legal maximum with a lengthened version of its standard underfloor chassis; the decision to opt for a totally new and untried layout was a brave one.

Two RE models were offered, the low frame RELL, intended for bus work, and the high-frame RELH for long-distance coaching work. In both cases the radiator was mounted longitudinally behind the rear axle and the constant mesh gearbox positioned ahead of it. The engine was the 10.45 litre Gardner 6HLX, with the 8.4 litre 6HLW as an alternative. There were plans to offer a horizontal version of the 8.9 litre Bristol BVW unit, in naturally-aspirated or turbocharged form, but this did not materialise.

Bristol chose air suspension for the new

chassis, following successful experience with Lodekkas and some MWs. British operators have never been completely sold on the merits of air suspension on single-deck service buses, and conventional leaf springs were offered as an option.

A prototype was delivered in 1962 to United at Darlington for evaluation. It was coded REX, signifying an experimental vehicle, but it was basically an RELL, and ECW had built an attractive service bus body for it; the body was very clearly an ECW product, and was the prototype for a style that remained standard throughout the RE's life, apart from cosmetic changes to the front and rear ends.

In 1963 a coach body was prepared for the RELH chassis, and the first vehicles delivered to various Tilling fleets. The coach body was well-built and attractively fitted out, but had a rather oddly-styled exterior which lacked the subtle simplicity of the previous ECW coach bodies on Bristol LS and MW chassis.

Production of the RE built up, and orders increased from Tilling fleets; the nationalised Scottish companies resisted the RE until considering replacement vehicles for Scotland-London coach services in 1966, when RELHs were chosen, and fitted with

*Top:* The 1962 REX prototype, with ECW 50-seat body, was delivered to the United fleet, and is seen here at Newcastle's Haymarket bus station.

*Above:* An early Crosville RELL6G, a 1966 example with ECW 50-seat dual-purpose body, using the bus body shell, seen at New Quay in 1972.

One of the shorter-length RESL6Gs, a 1967 model with ECW 46-seat bus body in the Eastern Counties fleet. Seen when new on the Ipswich-Colchester service.

Alexander bodies. By 1966 the Bristol RE was available to any operator. For the first time since 1948 Bristol was able to advertise in the trade press, and did so with great enthusiasm. 'What's so special about Bristol's versatile rear-engined single-deck chassis?' asked a 1966 advert. 'You couldn't get one — until NOW!'

And stories of the RE's excellent performance and reliability must have spread from the nationalised sector, for soon municipals and BET group fleets were coming in with orders. A further attraction was the option of the Leyland 600 and 680 engines. At the same time, semi-automatic transmission was offered. The range had been further extended to include two shorter chassis, giving an 'in-between' overall length of 33ft (10.05m); these were the low-frame RESL and high-frame RESH.

Many of the RE's new customers plumped for ECW bodies — like Coventry, Hartlepool, Leicester and Luton Corporations — while others stuck to their established suppliers. REs were built with bus bodies by Alexander, East Lancs, Marshall, Metro-Cammell, Northern Counties, Pennine and Strachan, and quickly confirmed their reputation for reliability. This was an important consideration, for several of the

rear-engined single-deck chassis that followed in the wake of the RE were far from reliable.

Shortly after the RE's introduction in 1962 Daimler exhibited a prototype rear-engined single-decker, which was revamped to reappear in 1964 as the Roadliner, with Cummins V6-200 engine. Then in 1964 AEC introduced its Swift/Merlin range, and Leyland the Panther/Panther Cub — similar chassis using existing engines. None of these chassis was an outstanding success — perhaps AEC's Swift had the best track record — and operators were desperately trying to find a suitable alternative.

With hundreds of REs running successfully in Tilling group fleets, in bus and coach form, here was an answer, and for a few years RESLs and RELLs became the favoured chassis for a number of fleets. In the north-west of England, for instance, Accrington, Blackburn, Burnley, Warrington and Widnes all took East-Lancs-bodied REs. In South Wales the ECW-bodied variety was favoured, with Aberdare, Gelligaer, Merthyr Tydfil and Newport all plumping for RESLs. Other municipal customers for the RE included Colchester, Fylde and Thamesdown with ECW-bodied examples; Lincoln with Alexander-bodied RELLs; and Reading with

Pennine and Strachan bodies to its own distinctive style.

Unexpected RE converts included several of the former BET group fleets, often with a strong Leyland background. Among those which took RELLs — not always with Leyland engines — were East Midland, North Western, Northern General, Potteries, Ribble, Southdown and Trent; many of these had ECW bus bodies, and several also took a variant with Marshall body.

Coach REs, usually the longer RELH, were also popular, but normally with the former Tilling fleets, with their long Bristol tradition. Many specified ECW bodies, but latterly several fleets took Plaxton bodies, and indeed some took a drastically improved ECW body which had more than a touch of Plaxton styling.

A further RE model joined the stable in 1968 — the REMH, suitable for 39ft 4in (12m) bodies. Full-length coaches have been built in limited numbers, and only three operators have specified REMHs. Eastern Scottish and Western SMT bought REMHs from 1968, and fitted Alexander M-type motorway bodies for the express services between Scotland and London. United also chose REMHs for its London services from Newcastle, but specified Plaxton bodies.

But it is as a bus that the RE really made its mark. And particularly when married to the ECW body. The combination of wide front entrance, low steps, wide gangways and properly thought-out body was unmatched at the time; the ride was good and quiet, and the performance brisk. The competition barely got a look in.

Why was the RE so good, when its competitors hardly distinguished themselves? It may have a lot to do with the thorough development that went into every Bristol model, particularly in its Tilling days. The RE prototype chassis were fully tested before they were bodied, and production only began when the prototypes had been evaluated in service. Some of the RE's rear-engined competitors were rather rushed into production to meet an identified demand, and this created problems for the manufacturers and for their customers.

So why was the RE withdrawn from the model lists at the peak of its success? The reasons are complicated, but are connected with both the RE's development potential and Leyland's working agreement with the National Bus Company.

The RE had been developed in the early 1960s, just as motorways were starting to sprout over Britain, and operators were looking for increased performance. A major revamping of the chassis, its transmission and braking systems, would have been

necessary to prepare it for the more demanding work of the 1970s. And Leyland and NBC, joint partners in Bristol and ECW, were hatching a scheme for a mass-produced city bus for the 1970s, which eventually emerged as the Leyland National. The existence of the Bristol RE and Leyland National, side by side, competing for the same orders, clearly did not make good business sense. So the RE disappeared from the British market around 1975, leaving its remaining customers to turn to the National. NBC fleets had steadily turned to the National from 1972, although a few coach and dual/purpose models were delivered as late as 1975.

Leyland kept the RE on the books for export customers, and this description was stretched to include the Ulsterbus company, which had a requirement for Ulster-built bodies, a condition the integral National could not meet. Ulsterbus has built up a fleet of more than 200 RELLs, which places it among the bigger RE customers. Top of the list is the Bristol Omnibus Group, with more than 400, followed closely by United and Crosville, each with 300-plus.

The Bristol RE made many friends in its artificially-abbreviated model life. After a shaky start, the Leyland National has proved itself a worthy successor. It is just a pity, though, that the only rear-engined single-deck chassis that operators really wanted was not allowed to grow old gracefully.

The ECW coach body for RELH chassis was a less effective design than the contemporary bus body. This was the first RELH6G supplied to United Counties, with 47-seat body. In Northampton when new in 1964.

The 12 metre REMH6G model was specified by Scottish Bus Group and United Auto for motorway express coaches. The Scottish coaches had distinctive Alexander M type 42-seat bodies, and a 1971 Western SMT example is seen during an overnight meal break in 1974.

Three of the rare RESH6G models, with unusual Duple Commander bodies, were supplied to Hants & Dorset in 1967.

Reading Transport had a sizeable fleet of RELL6Gs, including 28 with Pennine 34-seat standee bodies to this bizarre design. New in 1968, one is seen at St Marys Butts when new.

The attractive, spacious interior of the ECW two-door standee body on a 1968 demonstration RELL.

Luton Corporation bought 30 RELL6Ls in 1967-70, with ECW 48-seat bodies, and 118 is seen in 1969. They fitted well into the United Counties fleet when Luton sold out in 1970.

Marshall-bodied RELLs were bought by several of the former BET Group fleets. This RELL6L, seen in Matlock in 1978, was ordered by North Western, but was delivered to Trent in 1972.

*Left:* These unusual RELL6Ls were built for North Western in 1971, with ECW bodies contoured to pass under a low bridge. One is seen in Altrincham bus station in 1975, after it had passed to Crosville.

*Centre below:* An attractive 1971 RELH6G with 49-seat dual-purpose ECW body, at Victoria Coach Station in 1977.

*Bottom left:* When Bristol re-entered the open market, it started to advertise again. This ad for the RE appeared in 1966.

*Bottom right:* An RESL6L with 44-seat ECW body, supplied to Aberdare UDC in 1972.

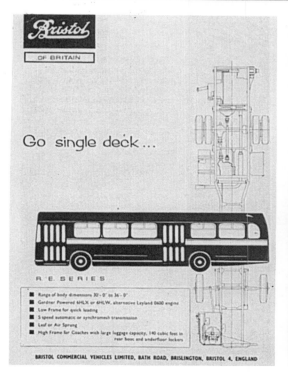

Go single deck...

R.E. SERIES

- Range of body dimensions 32'-0" to 36'-0"
- Gardner Powered 6HLX or 6HLW, alternative Leyland O600 engine
- Low Frame for quick loading
- 5 speed automatic or synchromesh transmission
- Leaf or Air Sprung
- High Frame for Coaches with large luggage capacity, 140 cubic feet in rear boot and underfloor lockers

BRISTOL COMMERCIAL VEHICLES LIMITED, BATH ROAD, BRISLINGTON, BRISTOL 4, ENGLAND

The later style of ECW coach body was much more attractive. This 1974 Red & White RELH6G is seen at Cheltenham coach station.

The then-independent Lancashire United bought ten of these RESL6Gs with Plaxton 41-seat bodies in 1974. One is seen when new at Eccles.

RELLs were supplied to Ulsterbus and Citybus after they were no longer available on the British mainland. This 1979 Citybus RELL6G had 50-seat Alexander (Belfast) bodywork.

*Right:* A familiar sight in Britain — an 11.3 metre Leyland National; this 1976 Trent example is seen in Buxton in 1978.

# Leyland National

Right from the start the Leyland National city bus had to overcome the inbuilt prejudices of many bus operators, for here was a highly-standardised, integrally-constructed city bus aimed at operators who normally had strong reservations about both concepts. Not that this was the case with every bus fleet in Britain; some, notably London Transport, Midland Red and the Tilling group companies, had preached and practised the advantages of standardisation and integral buses for many years, while there was a looser degree of standardisation in the fleets of the BET and Scottish groups, and little evidence of integrals. The municipal and independent operators often achieved standardisation within their own fleets, but usually it stopped there.

When Leyland and the newly-formed National Bus Company announced in 1969 their intention to produce a completely new city bus design, the bus business was going through an era of change. The whole industry was in a state of temporary uncertainty, and only a brave man would have dared to forecast just what market there would be for a standardised single-deck city bus at that time.

Against this confused background, Leyland and National Bus announced the formation of Leyland National Ltd, to develop jointly an advanced single-deck bus for world markets. This was not a new concept for Leyland, for there had been several design exercises along these lines in the 1960s, but the idea of cooperation with an operating group was certainly new. NBC's predecessor, the Tilling group, had benefited from an in-house manufacturing capacity, with Bristol chassis and Eastern Coach Works bodies, and the new link with Leyland was in many ways an extension of this. The Leyland National bus was shown for the first time in 1970, by which time work was well in hand on a highly sophisticated assembly plant at Workington, in Cumberland, designed to produce 2,000 buses a year on an assembly-line basis — a completely new concept in the British bus industry. Traditionally, most British buses were a marriage of a chassis built by one manufacturer and a body from a separate coachworks — often geographically distant from each other and from the eventual operator. Apart from the operators large enough to design and produce their own buses, the integral concept was never a popular one in Britain. Most attempts to sell integral buses to home operators failed miserably, and the separate chassis/body concept reigned supreme.

The hand-built prototype National was, understandably, the talking-point of the 1970

*Above:* The National prototypes were extensively tested — one is seen here on the pave.

*Left:* The testing included the rigours of the Finnish winter.

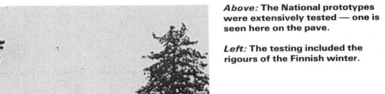

Commercial Motor Show. Here was a bus that departed from so many cherished convictions, and which represented such a massive investment that it could not afford to fail. Inside and out it was certainly different. Leyland's designers had set out to build an attractive, comfortable, safe and adaptable city bus which would satisfy current legislation in most parts of the world. With a rear engine, the floor level was kept very low, with a step towards the rear axle over the engine compartment. The wide entrance and low front step (368mm) was designed for easy boarding, and an exit door could be fitted forward of the rear axle. The small wheels, with low profile tyres, ensured that wheel arch intrusion in the saloon was kept to a minimum.

The choice of engine for the National was a controversial one. British operators tend to be unadventurous when it comes to engines, preferring to stick to well-tried units like the Gardner 6LW/6LX and Leyland 600/680 families. For the National, Leyland specified the horizontal 510 fixed-head turbocharged diesel, not only a new and unfamiliar engine, but a turbocharged one at that.

Passenger comfort was improved with the rolling diaphragm air suspension, and the ducted air curtains over the windows and doors; the interior temperature was controlled by an automatic unit mounted on the roof at the rear — the National's distinctive pod. The deep windows were designed to suit both seated and standing passengers. Various seating/standing configurations were offered. Normally the shorter 10.3m bus had seats for 44, dropping to 40 on a two-door bus, and 11.3m one-door and two-door buses had seats for 48 or 52 respectively. In all cases a high proportion of standing passengers could

be carried — up to 23 on a 52-seater.

The driver's environment was carefully considered, and ergonomic studies produced a cab layout which was logical and easy to use, with well-positioned controls and warning lights, and other aids like power-assisted steering and semi or fully-automatic gearboxes.

The safety aspect was an important element in the design of the structure which could absorb energy in the event of an impact, as dramatically demonstrated in an impact test at the TRRL, when a prototype was projected at 20mph into a 100 ton solid block of concrete, causing only localised damaged to the front end. To look at the body structure itself, it is necessary to consider the Workington plant, purpose-built at a cost of £8.2 million. Workington is an assembly plant, for very few of the parts on a National are actually built there. Instead they come from specialist suppliers into the stores area, from which they are drawn at the start of the production sequence.

One important consideration in the development of the Leyland National was standardisation of components, for although the bus was offered in two distinct lengths, 10.3m and 11.3m, items like front and rear end structures, doors, axles and power pack are interchangeable between buses of both sizes, irrespective of driving position or door layout.

All structural body members are first coated with an epoxy resin, for corrosion resistence, and the body components are then assembled in a jig, and the body shell is built up by riveting. The steel body is built on the ring frame principle, which gives great rigidity, and exterior panels are steel, with alloy below waist level for easy repair or

117

replacement. The body shell, with no body or mechanical fitments, is assembled, painted and undersealed before it is married to the units which complete the transformation.

The assembly line is quite unlike anything else is the bus business, and it is an impressive sight to discover how a set of components at one end of the plant can become a complete bus, ready for service, at the other.

Seven prototype Nationals were built in 1969/70 and Leyland subjected them to a rigorous four-year testing programme, including continuous running on pavé track and constant stop-start work; extremes of temperature were experienced in Finland and in Spain, and in essence the testing programme was very thorough.

A pre-production run started at Workington in 1971, and the first production deliveries commenced in 1972. The early customers represented different parts of the industry — National Bus, of course, came with the first of several orders for around 500 buses; the Plymouth municipal fleet specified Nationals rather than double-deckers; Selnec PTE, operating in the Manchester area, bought several for evaluation alongside the National's closest rival, the Metro-Scania model. There were early export orders too, from Jamaica and Australia.

At first the concept of rigid standardisation was closely followed. Operators who had been able to indulge their preferences when specifying other models found Leyland's apparently unyielding attitude on the National hard to take. It was not quite 'any colour so long as it's black', but some operators felt that it was just as restricted. The whole concept of Workington as a highly-automated assembly plant meant that deviations from standard involved time and money. In fact, the adaptability of the National was quickly demonstrated as 10.3m or 11.3m, one or two door, left or right hand drive buses flowed off the line.

Although initial orders were satisfactory, and the men at the Workington plant quickly mastered the new techniques, the National's early career was not trouble-free. For a start, the swing towards single-deckers did not prove to be as great as events in the 1960s had suggested. The low-floor rear-engined single-deckers, with seating and standing space for as many passengers as a double decker, were favoured for one-man operation before double-deck OMO was legalised in 1966. It was some years before the full effects of this were felt, with a massive swing back to double-deckers in the early 1970s, and an equally massive swing to double-deck OMO. With many large customers committed to double-deckers, there must have been times when Leyland wondered if their

investment in the National was really justified.

To add to the problems, some of the early Nationals gained a reputation for developing irritating faults, and quickly got a bad name in certain areas. In a project as advanced as the Leyland National, teething problems were almost inevitable. A new plant, using semi-skilled labour; a new engine which was not familiar to bus operators; preparation and construction techniques which were new to the bus industry. These factors and many more conspired to give the early National a hard time, particularly among operators who may have felt that the National was forced upon them, or who may have resented the lack of individual choice in specification.

With the benefit of hindsight it is possible to suggest that the National's intensive testing programme was all very well, but what it did not include was in-service proving with bus operators on normal stage carriage work, subject to all the abuses of drivers, passengers, fitters, the British weather and traffic-clogged city streets. The Tilling group had a policy of testing several prototypes of each major Bristol/ECW model in normal service with group fleets — a practice which certainly paid off with successful and trouble-free models like the Lodekka and LS. Leyland seems to have learned from its experience with the National, for the test programme for the advanced double-deck Titan, now in production after several years of development, included long service trials with London Transport and other operators.

National production at Workington settled down to an annual figure of 1,000 buses, roughly 20 a week, or half the potential output. The figure was far from unhealthy, but Leyland was looking at other variations to widen the appeal of the model. There was the Business Commuter in 1973, a design exercise involving a National fitted out as a mobile office/boardroom, complete with a mass of electrical and electronic gadgetry. More practical was the dual-purpose National, again unveiled in 1973, with coach-type seats, and a further development, the Suburban Express, with a high, one-level floor throughout. As a further demonstration of the adaptability, Leyland built the Lifeliner for the 1974 Commercial Show, a mobile casualty unit fully equipped for dealing with major emergencies, a highly competent project, but one which was not pursued. Since that time there has been a slow but steady demand for non-standard Nationals. Midland Bank has National-based mobile banks; British Airways has airside buses with wide doors on both sides of the body; the Scottish Office uses Nationals to transport top-security prisoners; British Rail is using

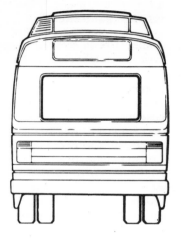

National body sections in developing a low-cost lightweight diesel railcar.

As production settled down, and the teething troubles were sorted out, the National's reputation improved and new customers came with orders. London Transport followed an initial batch of six with large orders, all for 10.3 metre buses. All of the British PTEs, over the years, have taken Nationals, and around one-third of the British municipal fleets include Nationals. Independent operators in Scotland and England bought small batches.

. National Bus, naturally enough, remained the biggest National user. By 1979, annual orders had brought the total to around 4,000, with examples in all but one NBC fleet. The National has become a familiar sight throughout England and Wales in NBC red or green, in a variety of sizes and layouts, on everything from close-frequency city service to gentler rural duties.

Export orders have been a significant part of the National's story. The most important order was for 450 for Caracas in Venezuela, but Nationals will also be found operating successfully in countries as different as Australia, France, Jamaica, the Netherlands, Norway and Trinidad. Some of the Australian buses are of interest as they were produced to an intermediate length of 10.9m using a mixture of 10.3m and 11.3m parts; the Australian Nationals were supplied in knocked-down form. An 'overseas' customer very much nearer home, and literally within sight of the Workington plant, is Isle of Man National Transport, which has taken several batches since 1974.

Minor improvements to the specification are introduced all the time, but the first major alteration was the Phase II model, unveiled in 1976. The batteries were moved to the front of the bus, and extra sound deadening was incorporated at the rear. The driver's com-

partment was improved, and the interior handrails were finished in black.

Then in 1978 came the Series B National, an economy version of the 10.3m bus, intended for less demanding work, and available for roughly 10% under the full price. The most obvious difference on the Series B was the absence of the roof-heating/ventilation pod, for a simpler heating system is fitted. Other changes affected the engine output, the tyres, interior lighting and external finish.

As National production continued, reliability improved, and later customers found that the stories about the bus which were circulating around the industry were not now true. With fewer single-deck chassis available, and long delivery delays affecting both chassis and body manufacturers, more operators were turning to Leyland, knowing that the National was now a well-proved bus, and that delivery dates could be guaranteed — and could be very quick as well. The fact that the plant's capacity could be stepped up to meet emergency orders has been appreciated by several operators.

This facility helped Eastern Scottish in 1977 when delivery delays created a vehicle shortage, and ten Nationals were supplied in a very short time; previously there had been

*Top:* **An early National in NBC service — this is Crosville's first example, delivered in 1972, and seen in pre-NBC livery. (It carries the wrong registration; it should be WFM 801K).**

**To evaluate the possibility of supplying National underframes for completion overseas, this bus was built in 1974 with an ECW body — an interesting combination of ECW and National design.**

no Nationals in any of the Scottish Bus Group fleets, and successful operating experience with the ten Eastern vehicles led to increased orders from the Group.

At the Birmingham Motor Show in 1978 a major change was announced in the form of the Leyland National Mark 2. The main change in the National 2 is the introduction of a bigger engine to replace the 510 unit. The 510 was not Leyland's most successful bus engine in recent years, and the L11H, derived from the familiar and successful 680 range, should prove more acceptable. In total, more than 6,500 National 1s were built between 1972 and 1979.

The prototype National 2 at the Birmingham Show retained the rear-mounted radiator of the original Nationals, but production vehicles feature a front-mounted radiator, and revised front and rear end panelling. Production of the National 2 started late in 1979. Other changes in the National 2 include a revised driving compartment in line with Leyland's double-deck Titan, and improved rear-lighting.

The Mark 2 brought an important change in the National's marketing strategy. When the Series B was announced, only in 10.3 metre form, it was offered as an economy version of the normal bus. With the National 2, the standard bus, in both lengths, will be the basic specification model, and operators requiring a premium vehicle will be able to order a full specification bus. The new front end added slightly to the National's length; the

Mark 2 models are 10.6 metres and 11.6 metres.

Another 1979 development benefiting from the technology of the National was the appearance of a Leyland-DAB articulated chassis, built in Denmark, fitted with a body built at Workington from National components — a successful exercise at a lower cost than a scatch-built body.

The National was received in 1970 with a mixture of amazement, welcome, scepticism and cynicism. Several thousand Nationals later the cynics have been proved wrong. Never before has such a highly-standardised bus been built successfully in Britain in such numbers; even London Transport's legendary RT type AEC Regents fell short of the 5,000 mark, while the National looks set to go on and on.

*Top:* To demonstrate the adaptability of the National, the Lifeliner exercise was shown in 1974, a fully-equipped mobile casualty unit.

*Above:* Another exercise — the Business Commuter.

*Top:* All of the PTEs have ordered Nationals; this West Midlands example is seen at Hampton-in-Arden in 1976.

*Above left:* London Country's large National fleet includes many of these 10.3 metre B series examples, distinguished by the absence of the roof pod.

*Above right:* The experimental battery National, converted from a standard Ribble 10.3 metre bus. Seen at Runcorn in 1976.

The distinctive nose of the National 2, here in prototype left hand drive 11.6 metre form, with an unusual three-door layout.